Tales from Peter~~~~~~~~~
and the Nene Valley

David Phillips

Copyright 2012 David Phillips

Front cover: Lyveden New Bield, near Oundle: unfinished masterpiece of the Tresham family (see *The Man Who Messed Up The Gunpowder Plot*, Chapter 2)

About the Author

Author David Phillips has spent most of his life along the banks of the |
River Nene. He was born close to the estuary of the river Nene in the
Marshland area of West Norfolk, and for many years worked as a
journalist in many of the towns along the river, including Daventry,
Northampton, Wellingborough, Oundle, Peterborough and Wisbech.
Today he lives on the banks of the middle Nene at Wadenhoe, in
Northamptonshire. He has edited fishing and motoring magazines and
writes regularly on countryside, gardening, motoring and local history
issues for local and national magazines. His other books include *The
River Nene From Source to Sea, The Adventures of a Pike Angler, Garden
Cuttings, Land Rovers Uncovered, Land Rover Adventures in Africa* and
Land Rover: The Story Behind the Legend. All are available as e-books
on Amazon Kindle.

Acknowledgements

Many of the tales in this book are based on stories originally commissioned
for the Local Living series of magazines. Many thanks to Joanna Borrett,
Nicholas Rudd-Jones, Fiona Cumberpatch and Abigail Richardson for
encouraging me to write them.

Preface

I've spent most of my life living or working by the River Nene. I was born near its tidal reaches in West Norfolk's Marshland and today I live on its unspoilt banks at Wadenhoe, in Northamptonshire. Over the years I've also either lived or worked in Peterborough, Wisbech, Wellingborough, Daventry and Northampton... never very far from the Nene's meandering course.

But the Nene valley isn't just about its river. It's about the people who have lived along its course and helped shape our modern world. Did you know that the meandering River Nene was the inspiration for that children's classic *The Wind in the Willows*? Or that the ancestors of America's first president lived along its banks? Well, it's true. Ratty and pals were created while author Kenneth Grahame daydreamed on the willow-lined banks of the Nene. And the forebears of George Washington lived by the river's upper reaches.

Wars were fought and lost along its banks, including the Battle of Naseby, a turning point in theEnglish Civil War. Mary Queen of Scots was executed at Fotheringhay Castle. But these are stories I've told before, in my book *The River Nene From Source To Sea*, first published in 1997 and now available as an e-book. It is by popular demand that I have written this book, as a sequel.

This book is about the people and places of the Nene valley and the surrounding areas, including Peterborough, Rockingham Forest and the Fens. Our river is more than just a gentle stretch of water that flows through our back yard. It's a place to be appreciated – and this book is intended to help you do just that.

Hopefully by reading about the places in this book you will be inspired to visit them, so I have included Ordnance Survey map references, particularly where they are part of a designated route or well worth a visit. I hope that adds to your enjoyment.

David Phillips

Chapter 1

Messing about on the river

Life in the Nene valley in the second decade of the 21st century is full of mixed blessings. We've lost village shops, pubs and post offices, hedgerows have been ripped out and fields concreted over as new housing estates and vast acreages of warehouses have sprung up. But one thing has got much better – the River Nene itself.

Throughout the first half of the 20th century, the Nene often suffered pollution from the industries that lined its banks from Northampton downstream. It also suffered neglect as the commercial boat traffic died and the locks fell into disuse. But the decline of heavy industry, tighter pollution controls and an increase in leisure boating has seen the meandering artery that has long been the lifeblood of our region gradually become cleaner and more accessible.

In short, The River Nene is enjoying something of a renaissance. Today, whether you're boating, canoeing, fishing, walking, watching wildlife or simply relaxing and enjoying a picnic or a pint on its banks, the Nene valley is a wonderful place to be.

There are so many ways of enjoying the river. If you fancy spending some time afloat, you can hire a boat, or take to the water in a canoe. This is the best way to explore the Nene, because you get to see the places far from the crowds, where your nearest company is likely to be a startled moorhen or a bemused cow.

The whole river is navigable from Northampton to Peterborough and the Nene is also connected to the country's extensive canal system (at Northampton) and the Fen drains and the River Great Ouse (via Stanground lock). If you've got the time – and the inclination – you can travel by boat from Peterborough to London, Birmingham or beyond by boat.

More practical for many, however, would be to hire a boat for a weekend. Modern narrowboats – based upon the traditional shape used by the commercial bargemen of old – are homes from home, with all mod cons. Mooring up by a riverside meadow full of wild flowers and falling asleep lulled by the sound of waterfowl and the lapping of water under your window is priceless.

You don't have to travel on the water, of course. You can also appreciate the river from its banks. There are plenty of footpaths along the Nene, because as a navigable river there used to be towpaths for the horses that towed the barges in the 19th century. There is also the long-distance Nene Way footpath, which starts near the source of the Nene at the village of Badby, near Daventry, and continues all the way to the mouth of the river at Sutton Bridge. For great views of the valley, you can't beat the circular walk that takes in Wadenhoe-Aldwincle-Thorpe Waterville-Achurch-Wadenhoe. Other great viewpoints are from the top of the old castle mound at Fothinghay and from the minor road between Barnwell and Polebrook.

On a riverside walk you're likely to see lots of species of waterbirds, including duck, geese, herons and swans as well as rarer species like the curlew, kingfisher and great crested grebe. White egrets – once continental cousins of our heron – have colonised southern England and are becoming increasingly common along the Nene valley. Dragon and damsel flies are commonplace in summer, darting about the profusion of water plants that grow in the margins of the river. Early in the morning you may meet a muntjac deer drinking by the water's edge, or a fox returning home after a night's hunting. If you're very lucky you may spot an elusive otter.

Some of the flooded former gravel pits along the river are now nature reserves, where you're likely to see plenty of wildfowl and waders. The Titchmarsh reserve (access via Aldwincle) has well-equipped hides as well as boardwalks to keep your feet dry in inclement weather when the surrounding reedbeds get flooded.

For many, the less strenuous pastime of angling is the best way to appreciate the river. Most stretches of the river are controlled by local fishing clubs, which offer either day tickets or cheap membership. Ask at fishing tackle shops in the area. Anyone over the age of 12 also must buy a fishing licence, which is available from post offices as well as online from the Environment Agency.

The Nene is famous for its stocks of bream, roach, chub and perch, with the occasional pike and carp putting in an appearance. Many of the riverside gravel pits are also full of fish – including Barnwell Country Park, which is famous for its large stocks of tench, and Bluebell Lakes near Tansor, where some of the UK's biggest carp are reputed to live. Day tickets are available at both.

The laziest way to appreciate the lovely river valley between Wansford and Peterborough is to take the train – the Nene Valley Railway, to be exact. This seven-mile stretch of track, which follows the river practically its entire length, is all that's left of the 48 miles of the old Peterborough to Northampton branch line, axed by the infamous Dr Richard Beeching, chairman of the British Transport Commission, back in 1963... although in fact Beeching was merely the person who wrote the report.

The real villain who signed the death warrant of much of our railway system was Beeching's boss, the Minister of Transport, Ernest Marples – a man who had a vested interest in getting rid of the trains because of his connections with the motorway construction industry. But that's a story I've already told elsewhere (The e-book edition of *The River Nene From Source to Sea*). A decade later, and wanted for fraud, Marples fled the UK in disgrace. He died in exile in Monaco, in 1978.

Still, at least the NVR's volunteers have made sure we can still enjoy a lovely fragment of the line. Chugging along the side of the river behind an old steam train is a lovely way to spend a summer's day. You can catch trains from Wansford, Peterborough, or the halts in between. (For details, contact the Nene Valley Railway on 01780 784444. Website: www.nvr.org.uk)

Despite the fact that the River Nene was canalised for navigation back in the 18th Century and is today controlled by locks and sluices, Mother Nature hasn't given up altogether on our river. It is still prone to floods, especially when heavy rain falls in the uplands of Northamptonshire at its sources. The last big floods were in autumn 1991 and spring 1998, the latter seeing several properties in Wansford and elsewhere flooded in a matter of minutes as a wall of water surged downstream.

Our ancestors knew all too well of the perils of living close to a river, so they wisely avoided building their homes on floodplains (a lesson our modern developers and planners could gainfully re-learn). As a result, you won't find many pubs adjacent to the river, except in those places where the natural contours of the land slope rapidly down to the water. Such a place is my home village of Wadenhoe, near Oundle, where the north bank of the Nene skirts a big limestone outcrop. Here, the 16th Century King's Head is on a steep slope above the river and hasn't flooded in over 500 years, although its willow-lined grassy paddock several feet below is regularly inundated. It's a popular beauty spot, where the traditional narrowboats moor up before negotiating the nearby locks.

You have to travel several more miles before the next pub on the river – the Queen's Head, at Nassington, which again has a good reputation for food and drink. In Peterborough, you can enjoy a drink and meal actually on the Nene itself, at Charters – an old coaster that was sailed inland to be converted into what is now a popular drinking and dining venue, close to the town bridge. Its range of real ales is unsurpassed. There really is a lot to do on and around the River Nene.

Some useful contacts
Narrowboat hire: Nene Valley Boats, Barnwell Road, Oundle PE8 5PB. Tel: 01832 272585. Website: www.nenevalleyboatholidays.com
Canoe hire: Canoe2, Ditchford Lock, near Irthlingborough NN8 1RL. Tel: 01604 832115. Website: www.canoe2.co.uk
Fishing permits: Leo Saddlery, 15c Market Place, Oundle PE8 4BA. Tel: 01832 275699.
Fishing tackle: Sheltons of Peterborough, 67 South Street, Stanground PE2 8EX. Tel: 01733 565287. Website: www.sheltonsfishing.co.uk

Working on the river

Those of us fortunate to live in the lush valley of the River Nene know that it's a very special place. But few of us love it so much that we would be prepared to sell up everything and start a new life living – and making a living – along its meandering course. But that's what farmer John Todd did. After spending a couple of idyllic summer holidays afloat on the Nene's willow-lined waters, he decided to sell off his smallholding at Weldon and begin a new life on the river.

"I loved boating, but it cost £1,000 to hire a narrowboat for a week and I worked out that I could make a living working on the river and my boat would pay for itself," says John. So he took the plunge, buying a 68-foot steel hull, upon which he built his boat, which combines cosy living quarters with a much larger cargo area, capable of carrying several tons of cargo. To cut costs, he built most of the decks and interior from reclaimed wood – mainly old pallets. A traditional cast-iron stove heats the interior and provides hot water. The boat is powered by a 50-year-old diesel engine that versatile John restored himself. "The engine started life as one of a pair used to power a fishing trawler," says John. "It's a four-cylinder Ford 4D, built in the late 1950s and early 60s, which was also used on Fordson tractors and Thames Trader lorries at that time. It's only about 50 horsepower, but it's ideal for pulling a big, heavy boat at low speeds."

John's work takes him the full length of the navigable Nene, all the way upstream to Northampton, where the river connects with the Grand Union Canal, which in turn is the gateway to the entire inland waterways system. He often spends the harsher winter months on the canal near Crick, close to the Warwickshire border, or at Foxton Locks near Market Harborough.

Making a living can involve delivering large loads of timber, towing heavy barges for the Environment Agency or British Waterways, or carrying out odd jobs. In his past life as a farmer, John had to be resourceful and learned a full complement of skills including carpentry, welding, mechanics and building work. But, most importantly, John's found an inner peace working on the river.

He's also found love. Soon after he met his girlfriend, Rosemary Robinson, she joined him on his boat for a few weeks and fell in love with both the boatman and his way of life – so much so that she has now bought a 58-foot narrowboat of her own.

"We're a two-boat family," laughs Rosemary, who admits that her boat provides more spacious living accommodation, including a better-equipped galley (boat-speak for kitchen) and an all-important bathroom and shower. It also provides her with a livelihood. Farmer's daughter Rosemary is a trained horticulturist who has turned the roof of her boat into a floating garden centre, from which she sells herbs and vegetables to fellow boaters, as well as container plants to tourists.

For John and Rosemary it's an idyllic lifestyle, waking up in the morning to the sound of water lapping against the bedroom window and a family of swans waiting to share their breakfast. But they're both aware that it also involves hard work. Back in their heyday in the 19th century, Britain's inland waterways were the motorways of their time. They suffered a decline through the advent of first the railways and later road transport, but using the waterways is the most environmentally-friendly way of transporting freight and today they are enjoying a revival.

"Our ambition is to explore all of the country's inland waterways, but the reality is that we will travel to wherever we get the work," says John. "When you travel by boat you get to see places in a different way to how you'd see them on land."

"Wherever we go we'll have a wonderful time," adds Rosemary.

John and his boat are available for hire. Contact him by phone on 07813 208042 or email rosemaryrobinson270@gmail.com

Living on the river

Fancy life in the slow lane, with the picturesque River Nene as the backdrop? Meet a man who decided to spend his life afloat – and reckons it's the best decision he's ever made...

"I wake up every morning to the sound of water gently lapping and birds singing. I look outside and see the mist rising off the meadows and the sun shining through the willows. It's utter tranquillity and I have it all to myself." So says Chris Bailey, whose idyllic start to the day is on the River Nene, where he moors the narrowboat he calls home. It's currently at Titchmarsh Mill, but next week it could be at Oundle, Wadenhoe... or whichever riverside beauty spot he decides to tie up at for the night.

You probably expect Chris to be a romantic drifter. Possibly an artist. Maybe a superannuated old hippy. But in fact he's a strictly short-back-and-sides man, who dons a suit and tie every day for his job as a civil servant.

"I'm pretty sure I'm the only senior driving examiner in the Driving Standards Agency who doesn't have to pay Council Tax," laughs Chris. "And I must be the only one who doesn't live on dry land. But I wouldn't have it any other way. When I relax on my boat in the evening and watch the sun setting over the reedbeds, with a glass of wine in my hand, I can't help thinking that I could be living in a house on an estate just like everyone else – and I smile with relief. I love my life on the river."

They sound like the words of a man who has spent a lifetime afloat, but in fact Chris's nomadic lifestyle began just four years ago, when he bought his first narrowboat.

"I was married with two children and I thought it would be ideal for us get away for weekends, as a family," recalls Chris. "Unfortunately my marriage broke up soon afterwards and I decided to live on the boat full-time. It was one of the best decisions I've ever made."

But learning to live on a boat wasn't all plain sailing...

"Things you take for granted living in a house – like turning on the tap for water, mains electricity and sewage disposal – don't just happen when you live on a boat," he explains.

"You have to fill up your water tank regularly and use either the boat's engine or a separate generator for electricity. Sewage is pumped out at special disposal units, which are situated along the river, but it's not as horrible as it sounds! The most important thing is to be organised, as you have to cope with less space that you would have in a normal house. But by making maximum use of what space you have, you can live surprisingly comfortably. Everybody says it is like Doctor Who's Tardis."

Indeed. At the front end of the boat is a double bed, while halfway along there's a sofa which doubles up as a single bed. It's situated opposite the portable telly and the woodburning stove that keeps the whole boat cosy in winter. Towards the rear is a decent-sized kitchen, complete with gas-powered hob and oven and plenty of work surfaces. There's also a gas-powered fridge, while concealed in one of the many fitted cupboards is a portable washing machine. Finally, there's the smallest room – a toilet complete with flush loo.

The advantages of living afloat are many. Besides that stunning view when you wake up in the morning, there's the bonus of being able to change that view whenever the fancy takes you. It's just a case of untying the mooring ropes and heading off for pastures new.

Holidays also come cheap. You take youyraccommodation with you. Chris has already explored the River Ouse and the interconnected Fenland waterways of the Middle Level system and one of his ambitions for the future is to head for Northampton and then travel the Grand Union Canal to London and the River Thames.

There's also the bonus of being able to move easily if you fall out with your neighbours, although Chris says that is extremely rare.
"Boaters by and large are the nicest people you'll ever meet," he claims. "They are invariably friendly and will do anything to help fellow boaters. If you're having problems, there's always somebody who'll help out."

In these credit crunch times, living afloat also makes financial sense. You don't pay Council Tax and even the biggest, most luxurious narrowboats are much cheaper to buy than houses.

"The only running costs are the fuel you use and the annual navigation fee you pay to the Environment Agency, which is £350. I also pay £150 insurance," says Chris.

Postscript: Chris has now retired from the Civil Service and has also bought a small house on the Greek island of Crete, where he spends his winters, before returning to England every year to spend his summers afloat on the Nene. "As far as I'm concerned, I have the perfect, idyllic lifestyle," says Chris. "The only thing missing in my life is a woman to share it with, but I expect that one day I will meet somebody with the same spirit of adventure. But they must love boats!"

Port Peterborough

Peterborough's town bridge is one of the city's beauty spots. It's a place where people go to dine in a floating restaurant, drink in a floating pub, take a trip to the Key Theatre or simply enjoy feeding the ducks along the pleasant, leafy embankment. But it was very nearly a very different place.

If the politicians of the 1930s had had their way, this area would now be a bustling port with oil refineries, timber yards, cranes and big, ocean-going freighters moored in a complex of docks. Millions of pounds were spent to turn Peterborough into an inland port. And the fact that those ambitious plans eventually came a cropper is down to fate and a certain Adolf Hitler. Let me explain...

The River Nene, which flows through Peterborough, has long been a working river – an artery of commerce from Northampton, where it is connected to the canal system, all the way downstream to the sea. Peterborough is 30 miles inland from the salty waters of the Wash, but for centuries that didn't stop local merchants envying the success of the city's downstream neighbour Wisbech – the self-styled capital of the Fens – which had built its prosperity upon coastal trade with the big ports in the north-east of England as well as mainland Europe and the Baltic.

Goods destined for Peterborough had to be unloaded at Wisbech and transferred to much smaller, horse-drawn barges – known as fenland lighters – to navigate the treacherous sandbanks and shallows of the Nene. It made incoming goods like coal and outgoing produce like corn prohibitively expensive. If only the river could be deeper, wider and straighter, Peterborough would be able to cut out the middle men and be much more competitive...

That dream began to look more realistic from the 18th century, when drainage of the Fens saw the channel of the river improved. In order to turn the bogs and meres into profitable agricultural land, excess water had to be hurried down to the sea as quickly as possible. The River Nene, which once meandered through the Fens, was diverted down a new, straight channel between Peterborough and Guyhirn, and the rest of the river's course to Wisbech and the Wash was also embanked and dredged.

Tides now pushed inland as far as Orton, upstream of Peterborough, and the tang of salt on the air made the businessmen of the day all the more determined to establish the city as a port. Various schemes through the 19th century were proposed, and some gained parliamentary consent, but the conflict of navigation and drainage interests through the length of the river meant that nothing ever happened.

During the reign of Queen Victoria, Peterborough became a major railway centre. One would have expected this new, rapid form of transport to kill off the inland port idea for ever, yet this wasn't the case. In the 1890s, the River Nene Navigation Defence Association was set up to renew pressure for the water link, arguing that it would end the railways' monopoly on freight transport. It wasn't until 1931 and the formation of the all-powerful River Nene Catchment Board that action finally was taken.

Instead of the fragmented approach to drainage and navigation of the past, the whole shooting match was under the control of one body. And that body was led by the charismatic former MP for Wellingborough, George Dallas.

Dallas was determined to turn the Nene into a commercial super-highway and he used all his political influence to get things moving. The river below Peterborough was dredged to ten feet deep and the shallow gravels at Northey, near Thorney, were blasted out with dynamite to provide enough water for big vessels to navigate safely. A tidal lock was installed nearby at the Dog in a Doublet, capable of taking ships 133 feet long by 22 feet wide and with a draught of nine feet. It was opened in 1938. All Peterborough had to do now was sit back and wait for the prosperous new trade to come steaming in…

Unfortunately it didn't happen quite like that. Although millions of pounds had been spent to make Port Peterborough a reality, the world had changed in the intervening decades. Water-borne transport was already in decline. The railways were facing competition, but it was not from the waterways but from motor transport on the ever-improving roads.

Dallas and his colleagues on the catchment board were embarrassed, but refused to accept defeat. They decided to indulge in a series of publicity stunts, persuading the Hull-based firm of John Harker to send a coaster, the *Constance H*, from Middlesbrough to Peterborough. At 36 metres long, it dwarfed the makeshift quay near Peterborough's town bridge when it finally arrived and was loaded up with 150 tonnes of creosote. It was followed a few weeks later by the *Peterborough Trader*, which carried away a cargo of 200 tonnes of bricks.

Local politicians were cock-a-hoop and their enthusiasm was matched by the local press, who predicted boom times ahead for the city. But six months later their enthusiasm waned a little after a reporter from the *Peterborough Advertiser* joined the *Peterborough Trader* for its return trip to the sea only to witness it going aground in shallow water upstream of Wisbech. "A harsh noise of metal grinding on stone" made the situation "very unnerving", he reported.

Despite this, the catchment board predicted that there would soon be regular freight traffic on the river and duly made plans for the troublesome shallow sections to be dredged even deeper and new docks to be built downstream of the town bridge to replace the makeshift quayside that had been used thus far.

But they were thwarted by a new enemy, this time from mainland Europe. The outbreak of the second world war in 1939 put the new engineering works on hold as the nation geared up to fighting Nazi Germany and its Axis allies. It was also pointed out, somewhat mischievously by road hauliers, that a ship travelling slowly across the flat fenland landscape would be a sitting duck for enemy aircraft.

When the war ended in 1945, the world was a very different place and freight traffic to Peterborough simply didn't exist. Road haulage was king and even the railways went into decline. The writing was on the wall, but some still didn't care to read it. In late 1946, the famous broadcaster and writer Fyfe Robertson interviewed George Dallas, during which the blustering chairman of the catchment board insisted that 2,000-tonne vessels would soon be ascending the Nene to Peterborough.

In that same interview, Dallas also boasted that drainage work on the river meant it would never flood again. Robertson's feature appeared in the *Picture Post* on December 14th, 1946. Just two months and two days later, on March 16, 1947, the Nene valley was inundated by the worst floods in centuries.

Today, even Wisbech Port is in the doldrums, with new port facilities near the mouth of the River Nene at Sutton Bridge taking the lion's share of modern coastal trade. Dallas died in 1961, aged 83, outliving his dream of Port Peterborough. That was already dead in the water.

In times of flood

With all the modern talk of global warming and drought conditions, a visitor from another planet would probably expect the Nene valley to be a parched desert. But generations of people living alongside the river know better.

Throughout history, our local river has led a Jekyll and Hyde existence. Most of the time it makes a gentle, unobtrusive passage to the sea, but every now and again it is transformed within hours into a devastating torrent of angry floodwater, causing millions of pounds of damage and even claiming lives.

At the time of writing the last great flood was during Easter 1998. A day of torrential rain over the midlands saw the infant river in the Northamptonshire uplands swell into a tidal wave that swept down into Northampton, flooding dozens of homes and drowning two people. It then carried on downstream, joined by millions of gallons of floodwater from its tributaries, overflowing its banks and spilling out across the meadows to form a huge lake more than a mile wide in places.

At bottlenecks caused by towns and villages, it caused yet more damage. Houses and businesses were flooded in Thrapston and Wansford, among other places. For 24 hours, my own village of Wadenhoe was cut off from the outside world, as the flooded river and its feeder streams spilled across all the access roads.

When the flood reached Peterborough, it swiftly engulfed the low-lying meadows off the Oundle Road. Ferry Meadows became one huge lake, the golf course was flooded and even Nottcuts garden centre disappeared under the advancing waters. In the city centre, the Embankment was soon flooded and the floodwaters lapped at the door of the Key Theatre. It was only below Peterborough that the huge floods storage area known as the Nene Washes were able to absorb the countless millions of gallons of floodwater, with the fields between Thorney and Whittlesey submerged for several days until the sluices were opened and the water allowed to escape to sea.

That great flood was in spring 1998. But you never know when floods are going to strike the Nene Valley. In the last century, the greatest flood of all was in March 1947, when months of sub-freezing weather were followed by a rapid thaw and torrential rain. Across the region, the meltwater combined with the rainfall to race across the frozen ground and straight into the rivers. Downstream, the problem was exacerbated by huge spring tides and northerly winds, which brought millions of gallons of saltwater rushing upstream into the Nene estuary.

Only the existence of the huge Dog in a Doublet sluice a few miles below Peterborough – built just nine years earlier – prevented a catastrophic flood from sweeping into the heart of the city.

Although the Nene is one of the slowest-flowing rivers in the country, with its flow controlled by man-made sluices from Northampton all the way to the sea, it is also the ultimate soakaway for every drop of rain that falls between the Northamptonshire-Oxfordshire border and the sea. Its catchment area is massive and stretches to the borders of Warwickshire, Leicestershire, Bedfordshire, Lincolnshire and Norfolk. When abnormally heavy rainfall strikes this area of eastern England, the Nene can struggle to cope.

Attempting to keep the Nene within its banks is the duty of the Environment Agency. But when adverse conditions do occur, it has no alternative than to open all the lock gates wide and allow the floodwaters to rush downstream. And although the Environment Agency can't do anything about the freak weather conditions that cause floods, it can minimise the impact. The agency's budget for flood defences in the UK is a staggering £500 million. And although most of that is spent on coastal defences, a significant proportion has been spent on the moody River Nene since that devastating flood in 1998.

In areas where floodwater is likely to inundate homes and businesses, great earth banks have been built to keep it at bay. In the last couple of years, a large new housing estate has built at Thrapston on former industrial land that has regularly been under water in the past. The EA hopes the town's new flood defences will keep those homes dry.

"We advise when planning applications are made, but we have no powers of veto," says the EA's Rita Penman. "At the end of the day, planning decisions are made by local authorities."

But what the EA has also done since 1998 is set up a feature-packed website (www.environment-agency.gov.uk) with the very latest information on flood warnings, as well as what to do in the event of a flood. For those who aren't on the internet, there's also a phone line: 01733 464357. "If you live in an area at risk from floods, you can also register with us for phone calls if a flood is likely. It means you get a call on your mobile and can take the necessary steps," says Rita. Those steps include keeping valuable documents upstairs. The EA also advises householders to have a contingency plan in the event of a flood, as time is of the essence when the floodwaters come.

That means moving furniture and other valuables upstairs and piling up the sandbags, if necessary. Although local councils will provide sandbags during floods, it is often too late by the time they arrive. If you live in an area where floods are likely, it's better to have your own on standby – they're simply bags (Hessian sacks are best) filled with ordinary sand from the builder's yard or DIY store. And they can make the difference between staying dry and the misery of dirty water pouring into your home.

The Environment Agency website also has an interactive map that shows whether your home is at risk from flooding. It's worth taking this information seriously, because although the Environment Agency does everything it can to reduce the risks of flooding, it can't control the weather.

Although the floods of 1998 were devastating, there have been others much worse in the past. In 1570 a massive flood devastated the Nene valley, destroying the bridge at Oundle in the process. Another, in 1793, was even worse, washing away the solidly-built stone bridges at Wansford and Thrapston. There is no account of how many lives were lost in those cataclysmic events, but it is likely to have been high.

It is not by accident that most of the older settlements along the Nene valley are generally built on higher land rather on the low-lying flood meadows.

And it's not just in the dim and distant past that huge floods occurred. In August 1912, a day of relentless thunderstorms across Northamptonshire and Cambridgeshire saw the River Nene rise 17ft 6in and flood parts of Peterborough city centre as well as the towns and villages all along the valley.

Unfortunately, the future isn't rosy. The whole of East Anglia is literally disappearing into the sea. Land levels are falling at the rate of 1cm a year as sea levels rise. It won't be in our lifetimes, but even the best efforts of the Environment Agency won't be able to prevent Peterborough-on-sea becoming a reality in the distant future. Certainly, flooding is something that is likely to get worse in the years to come.

Wayne's Underwater World

Beneath the languid waters of the River Nene lurks a world of savagery. And it has been captured on film. Wayne Hyde is director and producer of two feature-length DVDs that show the fascinating underwater world of our local river as it meanders through the Northamptonshire countryside. But the real stars are the fish – chub, carp, pike and perch, with a supporting cast of roach, eels, bream, minnows and crayfish.

Wayne, a chimney sweep from Rothwell, Northamptonshire, films them all. It's hishobby and he's a firm fixture on the banks of the Nene and its tributaries, where he sits and waits while his submerged video cameras record the action. I bumped into him on the river below Wadenhoe Mill, where he told me how it all began. "Five years ago I decided to capture on film the unspoilt local streams and brooks," he recalls. "It was just a hobby – I wanted to create a record of our fast-disappearing waterways. One summer's day, I stood on a footbridge over a stream watching four or five small trout in about a foot of crystal-clear water and thought how wonderful it would be to film them underwater."

The obvious problem was how to use a submerged video camera. Wayne's early efforts involved putting small cameras in modified plastic Ferrero Rocher chocolate containers. "The plastic was the right size and very clear, with no apparent distortions, but the two halves had to be very carefully fitted together and made watertight," says Wayne.

"The results were very good, but the system wasn't perfect and water leaks ruined two cameras in three weeks." After a lot of experimentation, he created a foolproof new housing made from a length of plastic piping. It was so successful that he built three of them, which he attaches to lengths of string and places at strategic points in the river.

"The Nene is teeming with fish, but what appears to be crystal-clear water is often not the case three or four feet below the surface. Below four feet everything looks dark green. Shallow water is best."

Having found the best spots, Wayne tempts the fish close to his lenses by throwing in tasty titbits for them to feed on – including dog food, tinned peas and fat-balls (the sort you hang up in the garden for wild birds).

"Chub in particular are very greedy and sometimes you get a whole shoal of them jostling for the food. They're not at all camera-shy! This is something anybody can do. There is no science involved – just trial and error. Any type of digital video camera will do – I have used JVC and Canon models with the same success. The important thing is to get the camera to fit snugly in the housing, which must be completely water-tight. Water damage is not covered by the camera manufacturers' guarantees!"

In the last three years, Wayne has lost or damaged five cameras – including one that he dropped off a bridge when a large dog crept up behind him and snarled in his ear. "It was a quite ferocious German Shepherd and I dropped the camera in fright... never to see it again!" he recalls. On another occasion, while paddling in shallow water to distribute his fish food, he claims he was attacked by a big pike. "It was at least three feet long and snatched a meatball as I dropped it in the water. My hand was only a few inches away from being part of his dinner," recalls Wayne.

But along with the disasters, Wayne has managed to film hundreds of hours of footage. The results were so good that he decided to edit them down to the best bits, add a soundtrack and produce two hour-long DVDs, entitled *Just Chub* and *Chub, Carp & Others*. "Everyone I met on the riverbank was fascinated by what I was doing, so my wife Larissa and I decided to invest in professional equipment to produce the DVDs. They are aimed primarily at anglers, so they can study the behaviour of the fish, but will also be interesting to anyone with a love of nature.

"I am also producing digital wallpaper versions – very gentle scenes which can be used as television backdrops at home or in dentists, doctors' waiting rooms, banks, airport terminals... in fact any place where people have to wait under a state of stress, worry or just boredom," adds Wayne

As an angler myself, I certainly found them fascinating. Voracious chub fighting between themselves to get to the morsels of food in front of the camera seem a far cry from the timid creatures that the 17th century writer Sir Isaak Walton described as "the fearfullest of fishes". Sorry Isaak, but the ones starring in Wayne's home movies most certainly aren't!

My favourite scenes are when the predators – perch and pike – move in menacingly… and the small fry do a disappearing act. I can't say I blame them: after all, who would want to appear in a movie where the big stars eat the supporting cast?

Chapter 2

People of Peterborough and the Nene Valley

It's people that make places, so who made Peterborough and the Nene valley? To find out, we must take a journey back through the mists of times. Nobody knows who first founded Peterborough, but there's no doubt that its position on the banks of the River Nene and on the edge of uplands to the west and the fertile fens to the east have made it a highly des-res for thousands of years. Stone Age people lived and hunted here and, of course, it was an important settlement 3,500 years ago during the Bronze Age, as can be seen at the world-famous Flag Fen archaeology site at Fengate.

The first name to be associated with Peterborough was Paeda, son of King Penda of Mercia, who in the year 655 founded a monastery here, which he named Medhamstede. In the centuries that followed, a thriving town developed around the abbey, which became very wealthy. But all that was to end late in the 9th Century when raiding Danes came up the River Nene and burned down the abbey. Then, in 1070, the rebel Hereward the Wake joined with the Danes in ransacking Medhamstede – looting, raping and burning down the town. His excuse was that he was preventing its riches falling into the hands of the hated William the Conqueror, but quite how rape helped his cause isn't quite so clear. Hereward was later – much later – portrayed as a freedom-fighting folk hero, notably in Victorian times by the flowery prose of the writer Charles Kingsley. But it's unlikely the people he terrorised in this neck of the woods felt that way about him at the time...

The Normans rebuilt the razed city and built a new abbey, twice the size of the old one, which was known as the Abbey of St Peter at Burgh (which later became Peterborough) under Martin de Bec, who was abbot from 1135-54 and did more than anyone to create the magnificent building that today stilldominates the city centre.

In the centuries that followed, a host of influential figures made their mark on the ever-growing town. It was certainly a golden age, with Peterborough's first historian, Hugh Candidus, describing the settlement as "built in a fair spot, and a goodly one, with rich fenland on one side and, on the other, an abundance of plough land, woodland, meads and pastures." Today, centuries later, I'd say that remains a fair description.

In 1541, as part of King Henry VIII's dissolution of the monasteries, Peterborough Abbey became Peterborough Cathedral. One man who witnessed all the changes of these troubled times was the famous Old Scarlett – the gravedigger Robert Scarlett, who died in 1594, aged 98, having spent much of his life as sexton at the cathedral. During his long career he buried two queens – Catherine of Aragon and Mary Queen of Scots – 51 years apart. His memory lives on in a portrait of him by the main door in the west front of the cathedral.

Peterborough grew slowly over the centuries. Although its cathedral gave it city status, it was to all intents and purposes an average-sized market town until the coming of the railways in the 19th century. Even political life was dull, with self-serving local landowners greedily clinging on to power. For example, a member, or nominee, of the Fitzwilliam family of Milton continuously served as MP for Peterborough for more than two centuries.

In the 1840s, Earl Fitzwilliam tried to thwart plans for a railway from Northampton to Peterborough because he had vested interests in another route, but happily the self-serving politician didn't succeed and the population growth that accompanied Peterborough's emergence as a major railway town brought a flush of new blood that would shape the modern city.

Frederick Henry Royce, who was born at Alwalton in 1863, started an apprenticeship at the Great Northern Railway engineering works in New England in 1878, prospered as an engineer and, in 1904, formed the Rolls-Royce company with Charles Rolls. They went on to make the most sophisticated luxury cars in the world as well as groundbreaking aircraft engines that would help Britain overcome Nazi Germany in the second world war.

From the same era and background came Frank Perkins, who took over the family ironworks in Peterborough to create the giant Perkins Engines Company that is still the city's biggest employer.

Although of no relation to Frank Perkins, his namesake Jacob Perkins was a celebrated inventor who went into partnership with fierce rival Joseph Baker to form the engineering company Baker Perkins, which moved to Westwood, Peterborough, in 1903 to build machinery for the food processing industry. Today it is known as APV Perkins and is based at Paston.

Peterborough has never been short of colourful characters. Step forward Walter Cornelius, who was born in Latvia in 1923 but made his name in the city in the 1960s and 70s as a publicity-hungry strongman and daredevil who won the world sausage eating championship in 1966 after polishing off 23 bangers in 10 minutes.

He also pushed a double-decker bus for half a mile, using his head, and ate three-and-a-half pounds of raw onions in two minutes and two seconds. But he will be best remembered by most Peterborough folk as the "birdman" who made several attempts to "fly" across the River Nene, flapping his home-made wings. He died in 1983. Walter's stunts were conducted from the roof of Brierley's supermarket, adjacent to the river and the town bridge, which would be packed with spectators, photographers and TV cameramen every time Walter attempted to defy gravity.

Each watery occasion was, of course, yet another publicity stunt by the larger-than-life supermarket owner Frank Brierley – the self-styled Pirate of the High Street and an entrepreneur who copied American retail techniques of the 1960s to bring cut-price clothes and food to eager Peterborough housewives looking for bargains. Unfortunately, it appeared that some of his wares had fallen off the back of too many lorries, for he was eventually convicted of receiving stolen goods and imprisoned. On release, he tried to rebuild his empire, but by then other stores had moved in. Frank Brierley bitterly protested his innocence, insisting that he had been "fitted up" by a corrupt establishment that want the self-made former market trader do well. He eventually died a sad man, in tax exile on the Isle of Man.

Another sad but larger-than-life figure who lived for a while in Peterborough was Allan Smethurst, better known as the Singing Postman, who had a series of novelty hit records in the 1960s, but had already descended into alcoholism by the time he was to be found all too frequently slumped across the bar of various city centre pubs in the 1970s. He eventually died in 2000, aged 73.

Prominent Peterborough folk have included entrepreneur Peter Boizot, founder of the Pizza Express chain and at one time owner of Peterborough United football club (which itself has been home to some famous sporting people in the past, including former England goalkeeper, David Seaman).

And then there was Andy Bell, frontman of the 1980s pop band, Erasure, which sold over 20 million albums worldwide. Born in Peterborough in 1964, six years later he and his mum moved into the house in Gunthorpe that my elder sister had just moved out of. Small world, huh?

More recent residents have included Warwick Davis, the actor who plays Filius Flitwick in the Harry Potter films, plus Aston Merrygold of the band JLS who took the X Factor judges by storm in 2008.

Peterborough's still got the knack of producing influential people, all right.

Roman Peterborough

The picturesque meadows flanking the River Nene between Wansford and Peterborough are one of the loveliest beauty spots in our region. As the river winds its tranquil course downstream between gnarled willows and beds of rushes, it's hard to believe that you're standing in what was once one of the busiest industrial landscapes in the country. But that's exactly what it was. Before Peterborough even existed, this part of the Nene valley was the powerhouse of Roman Britain. The landscape was scarred by quarries and vast complexes of smoking pottery kilns. It was the Stoke on Trent of its day. Iron ore was mined and smelted, fortresses were erected and influential Romans built great villas, baths and an amphitheatre here.

Less than 2,000 years ago, the important town of Durobrivae was built here, standing astride the greatest road Britain had ever seen. It was also the intersection of other important Roman routes, including the great Fen Causeway that picked its way between the meres and bogs of the flatlands towards the east coast.

The Romans were the first people to attempt to drain the Fens and turn some areas of the great swamp into rich grazing and agricultural land. They even dug a great canal from Lincoln to Cambridge to catch floodwater and prevent it inundating their fields of crops.

But why here? What was so special about this corner of the land that the Romans called Britannia? To answer that question, we have to go back to 55BC, when Julius Caesar first attempted to invade the British Isles. It was a flop, but he tried again a year later, succeeded, then promptly left to bask in the glory his conquest back in Rome. In truth, it was nothing more than the first recorded attempt by a politician to indulge in some spin-doctoring to bolster his flagging popularity at home. It did the trick, though, and Rome didn't bother Britain again for nearly a century.

In 43AD, the Emperor Claudius crossed the English Channel with a highly-trained invasion force. And this time it was serious. Over the next few years, the all-conquering Romans pushed their way north and, as they did so, they realised the Peterborough area was massively important. First and foremost, it stood at the border of the three main British tribes – the Catuvellauni of the south, the Iceni of the east and the Coritani of the north.

A great stone fortress to house the mighty Roman Ninth Legion was built at Longthorpe (where the current golf course is) and another at Durobrivae (near Water Newton) to guard the ford where the newly-built Ermine Street crossed the River Nene. The road was the greatest in the land – the main thoroughfare for the movement of troops and material between London and Lincoln. It was the vital north-south route of its day and the modern A1 follows much of its course, although stretches of the original road still exist, including a section near Ailsworth (Ordnance Survey reference: TL108 987).

The British climate has fluctuated wildly over the centuries, along with sea levels. Global warming is nothing new. In the early years of the Roman occupation, the climate was positively balmy, allowing the invaders to grow grapevines. Sea levels were also much lower and the Fens were much drier, allowing the newcomers to grow thousands of acres of grain on the rich, peaty levels.

To keep floodwaters at bay, the Romans excavated the Car Dyke, a catchwater drain between Lincoln and Cambridge which prevented the run-off from higher ground flooding the low-lying Fens. Stretches of the Car Dyke still exist, notably alongside the A15 on the outskirts of Werrington (OS ref: TF 187 033) and off the A47 bypass near Eye (OS ref: TF 218 016).

The heavier clay soil around Peterborough was less conducive to the primitive Roman agricultural methods, but it proved ideal for turning into pottery. The fields around Durobrivae (OS ref: TL 127 970) were soon riddled with kilns and the famous Castorware pottery was exported across the country, thanks to its proximity to Ermine Street. Examples have found by archaeologists as far north as Hadrian's Wall and as far south as Cornwall. The Nene valley pottery industry appears to have been at its height in the 4th century, only falling into decline in the 5th century as the faltering Roman Empire began to shrink and finally abandoned its British outpost.

That the Roman Empire lasted for well over five centuries is impressive. Just think: the British Empire lasted barely 200 years. Its success can be largely attributed to organisation.

The Roman army was professional and well-drilled, while its foes were invariably enthusiastic amateurs whose bravery and aggression was no match for the legions. Also, as part-time soldiers, they couldn't afford to indulge in long, drawn-out campaigns when crops were waiting to be tended in the fields.
The Romans also had the advantage of excellent communications. The stone-surfaced roads, arrow-straight wherever the terrain allowed, were a marvel of their age.

After the Romans departed, road-building in Britain became a forgotten art. As late as the 18th century, travel was all but impossible in parts of this region in the winter months due to the deeply-rutted, muddy tracks that passed for roads in eastern England. It wasn't until the age of the motor car, little more than a century ago, that we again enjoyed roads to compare with what the Romans had built.

Ermine Street was the best of all, but the Fen Causeway from Durobrivae to Denver, south of Downham Market in West Norfolk, was an equally staggering engineering achievement, involving the building of great banks to carry the road above the level of the Fens. A good place to see it is on the outskirts of Whittlesey (OS ref: TL 258 977).

The Fen Causeway was built no doubt to help contain the threat of the Iceni tribe, which had staged its first rebellion in AD47, just two years after Claudius's invasion. On this occasion, it was quelled by troops sent out from the Longthorpe fortress – incidentally, the best-excavated vexhilation (temporary task force) fortress in Britain, if not western Europe – who defeated the Iceni at their stronghold in Stonea, a few miles outside March.

The Romans later built another garrison at Stonea (OS ref: TL 449 927) to keep an eye on the tribe, but they hadn't heard the last of the Iceni. In AD61 a rebellion led by Queen Boudica saw Colchester and London razed to the ground and the Romans almost defeated. On this occasion, the Longthorpe garrison was all but wiped out. It is estimated that 70,000 Roman troops were slaughtered, and the Emperor Nero considered withdrawing from Britain, but the superior legions eventually defeated the disorganised Britons and order was restored.

A period of peace followed, in which the locals were encouraged to learn from their new masters. During the rest of the Roman occupation, the Peterborough area was one of the most prosperous in the country. This was helped by the plentiful crops off the drained Fens, as well as the pottery kilns and general industrial development of the area. Quarries around Wansford produced limestone for building as well as ironstone for smelting.

The foundations of great villas have been unearthed throughout the region, with the grandest of all at Castor – a richly-decorated palace where it is believed visiting emperors stayed overnight on their way to York. It is situated where Castor church now stands (OS ref: TL 125 984) and an artist's impression of the fine mosaic tiles recovered by archaeologists can be seen at Peterborough Museum.

In fact, the museum is a great place to start if you're interested in following in the footsteps of the Romans. Peterborough Museum's Stuart Orme explains: "We cover the entire Roman period in our archaeology gallery. We have artefacts from Longthorpe and the military occupation (including an original cavalry sword), a model of the Castor palace, Nene Valley pottery of course, a mosaic, a recreated living room and kitchen and items related to daily life and religion in the Roman period. This includes a replica of the Water Newton Silver, found at Water Newton in 1975 (the originals are in the British Museum), thought to be the earliest Christian communion set in Europe (about 300AD) and evidence of early Christianity in the area."

Stuart is enthusiastic about the Romans – and you can't blame him. Thanks to them, there's some fascinating history on our doorstep just waiting to be explored. Whether you take a leisurely steam train journey on the Nene Valley Railway (which travels through the heart of what was Durobrivae) or get your walking boots on and follow up the Ordnance Survey reference points I've given throughout this feature, there's plenty to enjoy.

On the trail of Robin Hood

Robin Hood was – and still is – the quintessential English hero. For 700 years we have loved the timeless tales of the one man who could deliver us from our wicked and greedy ruling classes. But did you know that Britain's most famous outlaw once roamed our local woods?

According to legend, Robin Hood robbed the rich to feed the poor; an outlaw from a cruel regime who, along with his band of merry man, roamed the forests that thencovered much of the East Midlands. This legendary hero of the wildwood was a frequent visitor to this neck of the woods.

Although the history books say that Robin Hood lived in Sherwood Forest, Nottinghamshire, there's compelling evidence that he was a frequent visitor to this area, particularly Rockingham Forest. Robin Hood was supposed to have lived somewhere between the 12th and 14th centuries, when Rockingham Forest was a royal hunting ground that covered 200 square miles, extending from Stamford in the east to Northampton in the west. Only 30 miles or so from Sherwood, it would have been an obvious retreat for the most wanted man in the kingdom.

Back then, two of the most important places in the forest were Rockingham Castle and the village of Brigstock. And it was in Brigstock's famous Saxon church that Robin Hood and his men attended Mass on Lady Day (March 25), the Feast of the Annunciation of the Blessed Virgin.

Local legend has it that Robin and his men were betrayed by a treacherous priest and, as they left the church, they were ambushed by a posse of armed men led by Sir Ralph de Hanville, an officer of the crown. Arrows flew in all directions and, among the casualties, were Sir Ralph and the treacherous priest, both fatally injured.

With blood on their hands, the outlaws rode off in haste and, a mile or so outside the village, Robin and his men got rid of the evidence by throwing their bows and arrows into an old, hollow oak tree before disappearing into the forest and posing as peasants.

The tree soon became known as the Bowcase Tree (later shortened to Bocase Tree) and would become a meeting place for important forest courts. Eventually the old tree died and a stone was erected to mark the position. Today, the Bocase Stone still stands in the spot, with the inscription "In this plaes grew Bocase Tree"… and a new oak sapling has been planted nearby to perpetuate the legend.

After the Brigstock incident, Robin Hood and company went on a hunting spree in the forest, poaching the king's deer. For a while they got away with it, but eventually the notorious outlaw was caught red-handed and thrown into the dungeon at Rockingham Castle to await trial.

Records at the castle do indeed reveal that a "Robyn Hode" was imprisoned there in 1354 for "trespass of vert and venison in the forest", but unfortunately there is no record of his eventual trial and punishment. Perhaps he escaped, just like he always does in the numerous Hollywood movies...

What other evidence of Robin Hood is there in the area? Well, there is the little matter of his early home. He is said to have lived in Barnsdale before he became an outlaw and most historians have assumed that was Barnsdale in South Yorkshire. But Barnsdale on the northern shore of Rutland Water has a decent claim, especially considering that nearby place names include Robin Hood's Cave on the road to Oakham and Robin Hood's Field, at Whitwell. Also, to the north at Castle Bytham, is Robin Hood's Cross.

Meanwhile, at Gunwade Ferry near Castor, on the outskirts of Peterborough, there are two standing stones, known locally as Robin Hood and Little John.

The true origins of the Robin Hood legend have, of course, been lost in the mists of time. The original tales and ballads of his exploits were passed down in the oral tradition and it was much later before they were written down and, no doubt, considerably embellished. But I'd still like to think that Robin Hood and his outlaws roamed our local woods, stealing form the rich to give to the poor. And I do wish he was around today, in 2011, to sort out those greedy, self-serving bankers and politicians...

Following in Robin's footsteps: You can get on the trail of Robin Hood by enjoying this four-mile walk which takes in Brigstock Church, the Bocase Stone and some lovely parts of Rockingham Forest. It is easy going and should take no more than two hours.

Start at Brigstock Church (SP946851) – note the 10th century round Saxon tower – then head north and through the old market place, bearing left then right (SP945856) down the lane. After 300 yards, take care crossing the main A6116, then continue down the lane for just over one mile, with woodland to the left and the open parkland of Fermyn Woods Hall to the right.

After Bocase Farm on the right, you'll find the Bocase Stone on the left (SP951877). After about 200 yards (SP949881), turn left down the path through Harry's Park Wood for about a quarter of a mile, then turn left (SP944881) and head south through the woods for about a mile. When the main forest ride bears left (SP944867) continue straight on along a smaller path. After about 100 yards, follow the footpath across fields and carefully cross the main road, continuing along path into village and turning left on the main street to walk back to the church.

The man who messed up the Gunpowder Plot

It is said (with tongue not always fully in cheek) that Guy Fawkes was the last man to enter the Houses of Parliament with honourable intentions. He certainly took the rap – and it's his effigy that is burned with glee every Bonfire Night when Britain marks the momentous events of November 5th 1605.

But the truth is that Londoner Fawkes was only a bit-part player in the intricate plot that was woven in Northamptonshire by local Catholics who had endured religious persecution at the hands of the Protestant ruling classes. Here in the Nene valley lived the men who almost pulled off the most audacious terrorist act to take place on British soil. If their plot had succeeded, the Protestant King James I and his Parliament would have been blown to smithereens by 36 barrels of gunpowder secreted in the cellars beneath Westminster. And the reason it didn't succeed was because a local man let the cat out of the bag.

That man was Francis Tresham, son of a leading local landowner, Sir Thomas Tresham. It was Thomas Tresham who had started building Lyveden New Bield, near Oundle, but had died on September 11th 1605 before the remarkable garden lodge was finished. He had already built Rushton Triangular Lodge, near Kettering, in 1597 as a celebration of his Catholic faith, with the number three – symbolising the Holy Trinity – appearing everywhere.

Francis, born in 1567, was the eldest of Sir Thomas's 11 children. He was educated at St John's College, Cambridge, but was not allowed to graduate because of his Catholic faith.

Embittered, he soon got involved in radical politics and in 1601 was arrested for his part in a foiled rebellion to remove the previous monarch, Elizabeth I, from the throne. He was fined £2,000 – an enormous sum in those days – which was paid by his father.

On October 14th, just a month after his father's death, he was invited to take part in the Gunpowder Plot by his cousin, Robert Catesby, the ringleader of the conspirators, who owned the manor house at Ashby edgers, in West Northamptonshire. In the room above the gatehouse, the 13 plotters planned their audacious strike. They were angry that the new king had failed to deliver his promises to be more lenient to Catholics and were determined to blow up both the monarch and his Government.

They rented a house in Westminster where Guy Fawkes lived as he assembled the huge arsenal of explosives that was due to be lit on November 5th when the king opened Parliament. And there's little doubt that it would have happened but for Francis Tresham's conscience at the 11th hour. Among the MPs who would have died in the blast were two of Tresham's close relatives. One of them was his brother-in-law, the 4th Baron Monteagle, who received an anonymous letter on the evening of November 4th, warning him of the plot. He handed it over to the authorities and the cellars of the Houses of Parliament were searched. Guy Fawkes was caught, red-handed. There is little doubt that Tresham had written the letter .

Meanwhile, the rest of the plotters were waiting in the Old Lion Inn at Dunchurch, just over the county border in Warwickshire. Once they'd received news of the plot's success, they'd planned to ride to nearby Coombe Abbey and capture the King's daughter, Elizabeth, and place her on the throne. Instead, they were themselves captured and taken to the Tower of London, where they were tortured, executed and their heads stuck on pikes for all to see. Tresham was also arrested, on November 12th, and taken to the Tower. He died there on December 22nd. It is thought he was poisoned, perhaps by well-wishers who didn't want to see him butchered – hung, drawn and quartered – like his fellow plotters. But he was still treated like a traitor: his head was hacked off and displayed alongside his co-conspirators, while the rest of his body was tossed into a pit.

Most of his property was forfeited and although his brother Lewis inherited what little remained of the family estates, the Tresham fortune was replaced by huge debts. There was certainly not enough cash remaining to complete Lyveden New Bield, which still remains half-finished, more than 400 years later.

Join the Gunpowder Plot Trail: Instead of burning a Guy and setting off fireworks on Bonfire Night, why not go on a Gunpowder Plot Trail, where you can take in Lyveden New Bield as well as the splendour of Fermyn Woods in autumn? Park at Lyveden New Bield (Ordnance Survey reference SP 985852), four miles SW of Oundle, and take the Lyveden Way footpath (signposted) south-west to Lady Wood.

Continue straight on the track through the picnic area until it reaches another path, where you turn left. After another quarter of a mile turn left again and follow this path east to Lilford Wood. You'll have great views of Lyveden New Bield to your left until you enter Lilford Wood. At the end of the path, turn left through the gate and back across the field to Lyveden, where you can explore the fascinating gardens, which have been restored by the National Trust to how Sir Thomas Tresham planned them, over 400 years ago. Allow an hour for the walk and look out for red kites, squirrels and fallow deer.

If you fancy visiting other places associated with the Gunpowder Plot, Rushton Triangular Lodge (SP 831830) is two miles north-west of Kettering, on the side of the road between Rushton village and Desborough. Ashby St Ledgers gatehouse (SP 571681) is just off the A361, two miles north of Daventry, and the old Lion Inn at Dunchurch (SP 486711) is in the centre of the village, beside the main A45. Today it is known as Guy Fawkes' Cottage.

French prisoners at Norman Cross

Did you know that one of the UK's biggest prisoner of war camps used to be on Peterborough's doorstep? The camp was at Norman Cross and, between 1796 and 1816, well over 10,000 French prisoners were held there – often in conditions that would be considered appalling by today's standards.

The population of modern Peterborough is well over ten times the size it was just 200 years ago. When the Napoleonic Wars were at their height, there were almost as many prisoners and wardens at the 42-acre prison camp as in Peterborough itself. In fact, the camp was a popular attraction for the inquisitive citizens of the city, who on a Sunday afternoon would stroll to the camp to see the "enemy" in their distinctive bright yellow prison uniforms – or very often stark naked after literally losing their shirts (and the rest of their clothes) in the endless gambling schools, for which the inmates were notorious.

Gambling was popular because there was little else to do for the bored prisoners – some of whom were incarcerated there for nearly 20 years. Each of the cramped wooden barracks huts on the camp housed 500 prisoners, who slept as tight as sardines in a can, in hammocks strung three or four deep.

The only water on the site was from seven wells, while sanitary arrangements were primitive. In such crowded conditions, disease was rife. In fact over 1,700 prisoners never saw their homeland again, dying of epidemics like typhoid, which claimed over 1,000 in 1800-01 alone. Smallpox, measles and dysentery were also rife. The victims were unceremoniously buried in a field, just off the junction with the modern A1(M) motorway. No trace of the remains have ever been found, which means the bodies were probably tossed into lime pits to hasten their decomposition and prevent further spread of the contagious diseases.

This all came as a direct result of the French Revolution in 1789. The overthrow of the monarchy in France put the anxious rulers of all the other European nations on red alert – and rightly so, for within a few years Napoleon Bonaparte has seized power in France and declared himself Emperor as he set about conquering the rest of Europe. All except Russia and Britain, that is. Britain's war against the French raged for over 16 years, until Napoleon was finally deposed in 1815. The military genius had made the fatal mistake of underestimating the Russian winter and the even greater genius of the Duke of Wellington and Admiral Lord Nelson, who gave him a good hiding on land and sea respectively, in the battles of the Crimea and Trafalgar.

Back then, of course, the French were the despised enemy. And during the long war we faced a big headache in trying to accommodate all those prisoners seized during the various battles. Existing prisons simply couldn't accommodate them, so the Admiralty realised it would have to build a new one. Norman Cross was chosen because it was close to the Great North Road (the modern A1) yet far enough from the sea to prevent escapees returning to their native shores.

Construction started in 1796. It cost £34,581 11s 3d – a huge amount of money in those days. The original structure, including the distinctive three-storey commandant's house, was built of wood, including the perimeter fence. However, the exterior of the house was later clad in brick and the camp was surrounded by a high brick wall. The camp was decommissioned at the end of the war, in 1815. Today, all that remains is the house, the old stable block and fragments of the brick wall.

The current owner of the site is Derek Lopez, who has spent the last 18 years renovating the house and turning the stable block into an art gallery. "When I moved here in 1994 it was in a terrible state," he said. "The house had been left to rot and was officially an endangered building. When I told Huntingdonshire District Council that I was going to restore it, they sent out two of their listed buildings officers and one said to the other: 'You see, wallies do exist after all!' I soon came to appreciate what he meant…"

But for Derek and his wife Mary, it has been very much a labour of love, with the couple getting to appreciate the history of the place over the years and being at the forefront of the efforts to safeguard its heritage. This has included the appeal to restore and rebuild the famous eagle column memorial, which was originally erected in 1914 by the Entente Cordiale Society (set up a decade earlier when Britain and France finally put centuries of wars and bickering behind them and became allies).

The Entente Cordiale between Britain and France came in 1904 and in 1914 the Entente Cordiale Society put up a memorial column to the memory of the 1,800 prisoners who died at Norman Cross.

The stone column, topped by a magnificent bronze eagle, was an imposing sight for people travelling along the A1. However, in 1990 it was vandalized: the column was knocked over and the bronze eagle was stolen, never to be seen again. Happily, the appeal for a new one raised £75,000 and the sculptor John Doubleday was commissioned to recreate the original, which was re-sited just off the A1, at the edge of the field where the dead were buried. It was unveiled in 2005 by the current Duke of Wellington, descendant of Napoleon's bitterest enemy.

The eagle, situated at the end of a layby on the Yaxley road immediately after the Norman Cross junction, is worth visiting. So too is the Norman Cross art gallery, in the converted stable block. It is situated about a quarter of a mile further along the Yaxley Road, on the left. Peterborough and St Ives museums also house many artefacts from the old prisoner of war camp, including some of the beautiful models that the bored prisoners made and sold to locals. They include amazing model ships constructed from carved bones and fragments of straw.

Last train for Northampton

Next time you're crawling along that slow-moving lorry park known as the A605 near Oundle, spare a thought for the motorists of the past whose progress would be halted every time a train traversed the level crossing at Thorpe Waterville. Today, such an event would cause gridlock, with traffic backing up to Peterborough. But, ironically, if that level crossing was still there today there wouldn't be so many vehicles on the road in the first place. Let me explain...

That level crossing was on the Peterborough to Northampton railway line, which opened on June 2nd, 1845. It was Peterborough's first connection with the ever-expanding railway network. But it closed on May 2nd 1964 – in the name of progress. A year earlier, the much-maligned Dr Richard Beeching, chairman of the British Transport Commission (but in truth merely the executioner acting for the dishonest Minister of Transport, Ernest Marples), announced what was arguably the biggest act of vandalism ever perpetrated by a British government – namely the axing of 5,000 miles of branch lines and 2,363 stations.

Our lovely local railway line, which followed the course of the River Nene for 48 miles, along with its stations that included Wansford, Oundle, Barnwell, Thorpe and Thrapston, were among the victims.

Until the arrival of the railway, Peterborough had been a sleepy cathedral city, with a population of just 7,000 people. But the railway age changed all that. More lines were added, including the vital Great Northern that gave Peterborough direct access to the capital. Almost overnight, it became a major manufacturing centre. The thriving and diverse city we know today simply wouldn't have happened without trains.

Yet that very first line from Northampton was built despite fierce local opposition. The landed gentry were among the biggest opponents – especially Earl Fitzwilliam, of Milton Park. Was it coincidence that he was the major backer of a rival bid to build a railway line from Cambridge? Luckily, the wishes of the vast majority of local people prevailed. When the line opened, the clamour for seats was so great that passengers even clambered onto the roof, which meant they had to remember to duck at every low bridge along the line.

Health and Safety wasn't a byword in Victorian times, yet the line had a remarkable safety record. There was only one fatal crash in its long history – on a stormy night in October 1877 when a goods train was derailed just outside Northampton. With one line closed, all other trains were diverted onto the one remaining line and a railway inspector inadvertently allowed two trains travelling from opposite directions onto the same stretch of track. They collided head-on yet, remarkably, only four people died.

Because the line followed the meandering course of the Nene's flood plain, there were no steep inclines and it was therefore a railway engineer's dream. Only one tunnel had to be built, near Wansford, and it was just 617 yards long. The entire line was built at a cost of £429,409 – against a budget of £500,000. Quite an achievement – but then, the engineer in charge was the legendary Robert Stephenson.

A railway journey to Northampton would involve catching a train at Peterborough East station, which was situated on the south bank of the river, a little upstream of the town bridge, near Oundle Road. The train would then stop en route at Orton, Castor, Elton, Wansford, Oundle, Barnwell, Thorpe and Thrapston as well as all the other stations beyond. Many of these were closed some years before the line itself was axed.

Remnants of the old railway remain. If you take the road from Elton towards Nassington, you'll arrive at a dip in the road where the long-demolished village station once stood. And on the right-hand side, covered with brambles, is one of the old posts that supported the level crossing gates.

In a field opposite the Fox public house at Thorpe Waterville is an old, abandoned goods wagon, while a few hundred yards behind the pub is the iron girderwork of the bridge that carried the line over Titchmarsh Brook. At Barnwell, adjacent to the A605 Oundle bypass, is the old waiting room used by the Duke and Duchess of Gloucester from nearby Barnwell Manor. The bypass itself was built along the course of the former railway line – and that was one of the curses of the Beeching closures of the 1960s. The infrastructure was torn up with indecent haste and the track bed sold off piecemeal. There was never any prospect of the lines being mothballed, just in case they were needed by future generations.

Happily, at the Peterborough end of the line, much of the old track bed remained. With the help of the Peterborough Development Corporation, railway enthusiasts succeeded in securing the last seven miles of the line to create what is known today as the Nene Valley Railway, which runs from Peterborough to Wansford and attracts tens of thousands of visitors every year.

A visit to the railway's headquarters at Wansford (just off the A1 at Stibbington) is a must for all the family. The collection of old steam and diesel locomotives and classic rolling stock is fascinating for all ages. Even the very young get a look in, with Thomas the Tank Engine ever-present.

By coincidence, on the day I visited, the man in the signal box overlooking the River Nene was named Ivor – a retired railwayman from Kettering who now devotes his spare time to helping out at this terrific operation, which is still run by volunteers. I'm sure if I'd have searched hard enough I'd have found a fat controller somewhere…

But although the Nene Valley Railway is a terrific place for nostalgia buffs, it doesn't detract from the fact that the real thing – the main line - has long gone with little prospect of returning.

Today, when you're enduring a stressful road journey from Peterborough to Northampton along the A605 and A45, you can't help but think how much more relaxing it would be to do it by train instead. So just imagine how travellers in 1964 felt when the line was closed: they faced a road journey before bypasses existed and which entailed driving through the middle of Elton, Warmington, Oundle and Thrapston, as well as negotiating a terrifying crossroads where the main road (the old Oundle Road) met the A1 at Alwalton. Dozens of people lost their lives at that particular accident blackspot in the years that followed the closure of the railway.

I have a copy of Beeching's original report in front of me as I write this. It's entitled *The Reshaping of British Railways* (it should be '*The Destruction of British Railways*'?) and runs to 148 pages, plus maps. Nowhere does it even attempt to imagine what impact it would have on the future of transport in this country. It was all about saving money – a quick fix that was expected to save the Treasury just £12 million a year. Pathetic, isn't it?

Successive governments – Conservative and Labour – closed yet more lines over the subsequent decades. Recent governments have talked glibly yet unconvincingly about us all abandoning our cars in favour of public transport… but what public transport?

In the rural areas of the Nene valley, there simply isn't a decent public transport system. But there used to be. It was the line from Peterborough to Northampton and it served all the villages along the valley. How I'd love to use it now.

Sinking of the Titanic: a Peterborough tragedy

On April 10th, 1912, John and Annie Sage and their nine children travelled from their home in Peterborough to Southampton Docks, where they boarded a ship that they hoped would take them to an exciting new life in America. But that ship was the ill-fated Titanic and, just four days later, it struck an iceberg in the North Atlantic and sank. Of the 2,200 people aboard, 1,500 lost their lives, including the Sages.

The sinking of the Titanic more than a century ago was the most tragic maritime disaster in history, but Peterborough has more reason to remember it than anywhere else in the world. The Sages were the largest family to lose their lives in the tragedy; and the blame for their deaths can be laid at the door of a slippery, conniving politician who started his career as MP for Peterborough. The name of the politician was Sydney Buxton. And if he'd done his job properly, none of those people need have lost their lives. But we'll come to him later. Let's first meet the ill-fated Sage family...

John Sage and Annie Cazaly were both born in Hackney, London, in 1867. They married on November 2nd, 1890. A year later, their daughter Stella was born, followed by George (1892), Douglas (1894), Frederick (1895), Dorothy (1897) and Anthony (1899). In 1900, they moved to East Anglia, first taking on a pub near King's Lynn before moving to Peterborough, where they opened a bakery at 237 Gladstone Street. More children followed: Elizabeth (1901), Constance (1904) and Thomas (1907). Two other died in infancy.

But John's wanderlust didn't end in Peterborough. Around 1910, he and his eldest son, George, went to Canada, where they worked on the Canadian Pacific Railway. It was by no means unusual. My own grandfather, William Phillips, worked on the Canadian Pacific at the same time (He may even have known John and George Sage, but he died in 1967, so I will never be able to ask him). Unlike my grandfather, who returned home to his native Hampshire to marry my grandmother, the Sages went on to explore the United States, which particularly impressed John – so much so that in 1911 he put a deposit on some land in Florida, where he hoped to start a farm and grow pecan nuts.

He sent Annie a postcard, which read: *"My dear, have found a lovely plot of land, Jacksonville is quite the most wonderful of places. I count the days until I'm home with my dear ones. Your loving husband, John."*

Meanwhile, George met and got engaged to an American girl. But both he and his father returned home at the end of 1911 to persuade the rest of the family to emigrate to the United States. It wasn't easy. His wife wanted to stay in England and their eldest daughter, Stella, had settled in Peterborough and made new friends. But John eventually won the argument, sold the bakery and paid off the balance on the land in Florida. He had the family's furniture packed into crates and paid £69 11s (£69.55) for third-class tickets for the entire family to sail on Titanic's maiden journey across the Atlantic. At their farewell party in Peterborough, John joked with friends and relatives that he would send them pecan nuts from his new farm.

How excited they must have been. The Titanic was the pride of the White Star Line and said to be the greatest ocean liner ever built. It was 882ft long, 92ft wide and boasted 29 coal-fired boilers to power the huge steam engines that could propel it across the storm-tossed oceans at what was then an incredibly fast 23 knots (26.5mph). It was the largest man-made moving object in the world – and it was said to be unsinkable. Nothing could threaten the Titanic, they reckoned. No doubt that's why the owners didn't bother to carry enough lifeboats for all the 2,200 people aboard. At that time the legal minimum for boats over 10,000 tons was just 16 – an astonishing figure which dated back to 1894, when ships were much smaller. It meant that the Titanic, at 46,000 tons, was legally obliged to carry enough lifeboats for less than half its capacity. Those 16 lifeboats could hold a maximum of 990 people.

Ironically, just a year earlier, proposed legislation had appeared before parliament which should have updated that inadequate law and made it compulsory for the Titanic to carry sufficient lifeboats. Incredibly, it was blocked by the President of the Board of Trade, Sydney Buxton. Since joining the House of Commons as Liberal MP for Peterborough in 1883, at the age of 30, Buxton's rise to power had been steady. In 1892 he was appointed Under-Secretary for the Colonies and in 1905 became Postmaster General.

A favourite with Prime Minister Herbert Asquith, he was given the important Cabinet post of President of the Board of Trade in 1910. By now aged 57, he made no secret of his ambition to eventually become PM himself. As head of the Board of Trade, Buxton was responsible for shipping regulations, but had ignored reform in 1911. He had stalled on the essential legislation that would have made it mandatory for ships to carry sufficient lifeboats for all passengers.

Meanwhile, as the Titanic departed from Southampton, the Sage family were enjoying the experience. Although they travelled in third class – known as "steerage" – their accommodation was better than first class on some lesser liners of the day. For most of the family, it was their first taste of foreign shores as they stopped to pick up more passengers at Cherbourg, in northern France, and Queenstown (now Cobh) in southern Ireland.

Among the other passengers on board was J Bruce Ismay, managing director of the White Star Line. It is alleged that he urged the captain, Edward J Smith, to head for New York at full speed, in order to surpass the crossing times achieved by his company's major rivals, the Cunard Line. This was despite repeated warnings that there were icebergs in the area.

The Titanic was south of the Grand Banks of Newfoundland at 11.40pm on April 14th when she struck the iceberg. Despite a calm sea, there was no moon and in the pitch darkness the lookouts in the crow's nest spotted the iceberg just 37 seconds before impact. It was much too late to avoid it and, although First Officer William Murdoch attempted to steer the ship hard to the left (port), a collision was inevitable.

The impact buckled the steel plates in the hull, tearing apart rivets and allowing the ocean to pour in. As the ship listed and the lower decks where the "steerage" passengers were berthed began to flood, the Sage family knew they had to escape. But they were in for a shock. Survivors claimed that third-class passengers were held back while first and second-class passengers laid first claim to the lifeboats.

Certainly, some of the gates that separated the third-class cabins from the rest of the ship had been left locked. The terror of passengers like the Sage family, trapped below decks in a sinking ship, does not bear thinking about.

Despite the tradition of "women and children first", the odious White Star boss Ismay elbowed himself to the front of the queue to join the lifeboats. He survived, while most of the unfortunate passengers aboard his ship were left to drown. It was later revealed that a greater proportion of first-class men survived than third-class women and children. The stricken ship eventually sank two hours and 40 minutes after the collision with the iceberg, at 2.20am on Monday April 15th. Those who could not find a place on a lifeboat but tried to cling on floating wreckage soon succumbed to hypothermia in the freezing (minus-2 deg C) water. The entire Sage family perished. It was reported that Stella did manage to get aboard a lifeboat, but left it when she realised that the rest of her family would be left behind.

The survivors shivering in the lifeboats were rescued a couple of hours later by the liner Carpathia, owned by bitter rivals Cunard. Among them, of course, was the pathetic Ismay. By saving his own skin and allowing others to die, he outraged the public and he was portrayed by the national press as the greatest coward of all time. He was ostracised by London society, who said that he should have held back and gone down with the ship. Ninety-five years on, I can't imagine many people disagreeing with that view.

Less fortunate were the Sages. The entire family of 11 perished. Only the body of William Sage, aged 14, was ever recovered. He was found by crew on the Mackay Bennett – one of the merchant vessels that steamed to the scene of the disaster, but were too late to save more than a few lives. The remains of young William were reunited with the rest of his family when he was buried at sea.

That a whole family – parents both aged 44 and all nine of their children, aged four to 20 years – had perished was a scandal at the time. Despite the years that have since passed, it is every bit as tragic today. These were our people, killed by commercial greed and stupidity.

I would love to end this story by telling you that the bad guys were hauled over the coals and made to suffer for the immense suffering they were responsible for. But it didn't happen. An inquiry by the British Board of Trade – headed by Buxton, of course – concluded that safety rules were out of date and recommended new laws. Buxton misled the House of Commons by stating that he had rejected new rules on lifeboats proposed the previous year because he believed they were "inadequate". In fact, if implemented, they would have provided enough lifeboat accommodation for everyone aboard the Titanic. For stalling on those life-saving measures, he should have resigned. But somehow he clung on, perhaps hoping that the issue would blow over and he would still one day become Prime Minister.

In February 1914, the hugely unpopular Buxton got promotion of sorts, but it wasn't what he'd hoped for. He was appointed Governor General of South Africa and banished to the Cape. In 1920, when the fuss had died down, he retired and returned to the UK where he was created an Earl. He died in 1934, at the age of 81. Ismay resigned as MD of White Star Line in 1913, but remained active in maritime affairs. In 1919 he attempted to redeem himself by setting up a £25,000 fund to recognise the contribution of merchant seamen during World War 1. But he remained forever despised for his selfish actions that fateful night in April 1912. He died in 1937, aged 74.

The Titanic's final resting place, 2,500ft below the surface of the Atlantic Ocean, was left undisturbed until 1985 when a joint American-French expedition led by Dr Robert Ballard discovered the wreck with a video-equipped submersible.

Dr Ballard and his team did not plunder the wreck, as they considered that such an act would be grave-robbing. But once its position had been pinpointed, human greed was inevitable. A legal debate over the ownership raged, then salvage work began. Thousands of artefacts, including personal belongings, are now part of various museum exhibitions around the world, including a travelling show that has appeared at Peterborough Museum, among others.

Opinion on these exhibitions is divided, with the grave-robbing argument always to the fore. But if that view was taken to its logical conclusion, archaeology itself would cease to exist. The only difference between excavating an ancient Egyptian tomb and recovering artefacts from the Titanic is the passage of time.

The pro-salvage view isn't helped by crass Titanic exhibitions staged in America. How about this one (quoted verbatim): "Enjoy Las Vegas entertainment at Tropicana Las Vegas... come and marvel at over 300 authentic Titanic artefacts... visitors can actually feel the weather conditions experienced by passengers on the fateful night..." Meanwhile, each visitor receives a random ticket as they enter, bearing a name of a real passenger. When they leave, they are told the fate of "their" passenger. Talk about bad taste...

Now where did I put that red box?

Next time you see the Chancellor of the Exchequer raise his red box aloft on his way to the House of Commons to deliver a new Budget, you can blame it on the giant of man who once lived in Wadenhoe House, Northamptonshire.

The magnificent Jacobean manor house was owned by George Ward Hunt, chancellor in Disraeli's first government during the reign of Queen of Victoria. And it was in his very first budget speech that he discovered, to his horror, that he had left his red despatch box behind in Wadenhoe.

As a result, chancellors ever since have raised that battered box aloft to the assembled crowd – just to reassure everybody concerned that they haven't left it at home.

Wadenhoe House hosted most of the famous statesmen of the day. At a time when Britain was the most powerful nation in the world, members of Disraeli's government regularly converged upon Wadenhoe at weekends. It was, in effect, the Chequers of its day.

At over 6ft 4in tall and weighing in at 25 stone, George Ward Hunt was certainly the biggest chancellor in history. He also built the world's first village post office – or postal telegraph office, as it was known then – in Wadenhoe so that he could be kept informed of matters of state while he was in the country enjoying shooting parties. Although it ceased to be a post office more than a decade ago, the old enamel "Postal Telegraph Office" sign can still be seen above the door of the building, now a private dwelling, in the centre of the village.

The Ward Hunt family lived in Wadenhoe House from the 18th century through to the 1960s, when it became one of the area's first conference centres.

A harvest of eels

There's barely a ripple to disturb the surface as the battered boat makes its way along the Old River Nene. Peter Carter is on his way to work, doing the same job as his ancestors have done for over 500 years. But today it's a job that's in danger of disappearing, for Peter is Britain's very last eel traditional eel trapper.

"We've traced the family tree back to 1475 and we've all lived off the Fens," says Peter, who, like all those previous generations, has lived in and worked in the endlessly flat landscape east of Peterborough.

There used to be scores of eel catchers, trapping the mysterious, serpent-like migratory fish – many of which were sent to the capital to feed Londoners' voracious appetite for jellied eels. But in recent decades eel stocks declined and eel catching was no longer so lucrative. Gradually the old eel catchers faded away and weren't replaced by a new generation. Except for Peter, that is.

The stretch of the Nene where Peter plies his trade bears little relation to the wide reaches that flow through Peterborough, for this is the old course of the river, abandoned more than two centuries ago when the main river was diverted down a straight new channel to hasten floodwater down to the sea.

Today, the Old Nene is a quiet backwater, but it is the perfect environment for scavenging eels, which thrive in the sluggish, stagnant waters, where they seek out their food – dead fish and animals – by smell. Not to put too fine a point on it, the smellier the food, the more the eels like it.

Peter uses this knowledge to his advantage. He baits his home-made wicker traps with roadkill – dead animals he picks up from the side of the road. The traps are left overnight in the river until Peter returns the next day to empty them of their valuable harvest.

Just like his ancestors, Peter uses punts and boats to bait and check his traps. But he does so in a very different landscape to what they would have known. The Fens were a vast and impenetrable watery wilderness until the 17th Century when Dutch experts were called in to begin the long process of draining it.

It was a tough life for the Fenmen of old – malaria was rampant in the steaming swamps – but at least there was food a-plenty. Millions of ducks and wild geese were there for the taking, while the waterways teemed with fish – especially eels.

"Eels were the currency of the Fens in those days," says Peter. "Villages would pay their taxes in eels. The stone that was used to build Ely Cathedral was bought with eels. There was water everywhere and every drop had eels in it."

Those rivers and drains were the highways of the day in the Fens, where proper roads didn't exist until the drainage efforts were stepped up in the 19th Century by Victorians, who used powerful drainage pumps to turn the damp meadows into arable land. Wheat and barley grew where generations of Fenmen had earned a living from catching fish and fowl.

But as the water dwindled, so did the eels – and the eel catchers. Most of the wildfowlers and fishermen turned to agriculture for employment instead, although the Carter family pressed on stubbornly, keeping the old traditions alive.

"My grandfather was one of 21 children, which was a lot of mouths to feed. They all had to do their bit to put food on the table and eels were both free and nutritious. Grandad was a successful eel fisherman and he did it all his life – and he passed his secrets down to me."

As a young boy, Peter hated school. "I was dyslexic, hated lessons and was always skiving off to escape into the Fens and be with granddad, catching eels. When I left school it seemed natural to be an eel fisherman and I've done it ever since."

But although he appears to have a very traditional lifestyle, Peter's life has changed a great deal. When he started his career as professional fisherman 30 years ago, eel stocks were plentiful. But they have plummeted by 80 per cent since the 1980s. Peter believes this is due to the modernisation of the drainage sluices across the Fens, with leaky old wooden lock gates replaced by efficient steel ones.

Peter explains: "Eels are migratory. They are born thousands of miles away in an area of the Atlantic Ocean known as the Sargasso Sea and the baby eels, known as elvers, are carried to Europe on the Gulf Stream. They then enter the river estuaries and swim upstream. There used to be lots of gaps in the old wooden gates for the elvers to squeeze through, but very few of them can get through any more.

"When I began eel fishing, I could catch 200 in a night, easy. These days it's a very good night if I get 40 or 50. It's a worrying decline."

The decline was enough to see off the few remaining eel fishermen – apart from Peter, that is. Like the countless generations of Carters before him, he trusted to luck in times of change and carried on regardless, looking for new waters in which to place his traditional traps.

Ironically, it was the modern age of technology that came to his rescue – namely the electronic media and its thirst for good stories. In 2006 he agreed to give a demonstration on eel catching at an exhibition at the Wetland Centre at nearby Welney. It was attended by HM the Queen, as well as the television cameras, and after that his phone hardly stopped ringing.

Since then, he has appeared on several TV programmes, including *Countryfile, Time Team, Escape to the Country, Flog It* and even the *One Show*, where he turned up at BBC Television centre in London with a bucketful of eels and a fascinating repertoire of anecdotes. He's rubbed shoulders with celebrities like Chris Evans, Julia Bradbury, Sheila Hancock, Griff Rhys-Jones, Ade Edmondson and Michael Portillo.

The small shop and workshop in which he sells eels and makes traditional willow traps - known as "hives" - nets, baskets and other traditional country goods sees a stream of visitors from all over the world. "People from America, Australia, Japan and even China have come to the UK on holiday and dropped in to see me because they've seen me on telly," laughs Peter.

He is also in big demand to give talks to schools, colleges and WI groups all over the country, as well as country shows. His life has changed in many ways, but he loves every moment of it. "Being a bit of a celebrity doesn't bother me because I love meeting people and talking to them," says Peter. "It also helps me keep eel trapping alive. People wouldn't know about this traditional way of life otherwise."

It has also brought other changes. For over 20 years he drove around in a battered old 1964 Land Rover, which was ideal for short journeys down bumpy local farm tracks. But travelling hundreds of miles to speaking engagements at 50mph in a draughty cab with a rudimentary heater wasn't much fun, so a year ago he sold it and opted for a modern Freelander, better suited to motorway travel. "My wife Sian prefers it, too," admits Peter.

Peter has embraced the future – and it's a future that looks brighter than it did a decade ago. The Environment Agency is now installing ingenious "eel ladders" at lock gates across the Fens to allow the migrating fish to clamber through the locks, so stocks should improve in the coming years. And despite being a media star, he is determined to continue with his traditional lifestyle. Says Peter: "I haven't got a son to continue the family tradition, but my teenage daughter, Rhianna, loves coming out with me in the boat.

"She's much brighter than me and doing really well at school. Her ambition is to be a zoologist and if she decides to do that I'll support her all the way, but if she eventually decides to be an eel catcher I'll be just as proud of her. If I'm lucky, I reckon I've got 30 years left. I'll never retire – why should I? I don't see this as a job, I love every moment of it."

Peter Carter's shop and workshop is at 8-9 Church Terrace, Outwell, near Wisbech PE14 8RQ. Tel: 01945 772157. Besides selling eels and traps, Peter also weaves baskets from willow that he grows himself – anything from a beautifully-crafted picnic hamper to a willow coffin, in fact. "I'm open every day apart from Thursday from about 10am to 5pm... but phone first to make sure I'm not out in the Fens," says Peter, who has published a booklet revealing the Carter family's eels recipes, passed down through the generations. These include eel soup, but Peter's favourite is fried eels.

Chapter 3

On the trail of our greatest writers

"The past is a foreign country; they do things differently there," wrote local author L.P. Hartley, in his famous novel, *The Go-Between*. But in the case of our area, both the past and present have produced a rich array of literary talent. Hartley is one of the best-known, but he's by no means alone: wherever you go in this area you're likely to be walking in the footsteps of great writers and poets.

Why not join me on a literary trail to some of the places that have inspired them? And as good a place to start as any is Peterborough Cathedral (OS ref: TL 192986), where our earliest great writer was educated. John Fletcher (1579-1625) was the son of the Dean of Peterborough Cathedral and attended the King's School, then in the cathedral precincts.

At the age of just 11, Fletcher went up to Corpus Christi College, Cambridge, and later became one of the great dramatists of his age, working in collaboration with William Shakespeare, with whom he co-wrote Henry VIII, Two Noble Kinsmen and a third play, Cardenio (since lost). He later died of the plague and was buried in the chancel of Southwark Cathedral, London, alongside Shakespeare's brother, Edmund.

Peterborough Cathedral also inspired our greatest poet, John Clare (1793-1864), who in the 1820s was a guest of the wife of the Rt Rev Dr Herbert Marsh, Bishop of Peterborough, who had taken an interest in Clare and invited him to visit her at the Bishop's Palace.

He was taken to a room, supplied with paper, pens and ink and expected to write a masterpiece there and then! Mortified, he fled to the nearby Red Lion pub. By the time he returned he was very drunk, but happily the Bishop's wife wrongly attributed his condition to "high poetic musings"!

Mrs Marsh wasn't the only person to misunderstand the celebrated "Peasant Poet", who was born at Helpston and, after a tragic life that included long spells in lunatic asylums, was buried in Helpston churchyard (TF 122054) where his grave has become a shrine to poetry lovers around the world.

Nearby is a memorial erected to his memory and the cottage where he was born, which is now a learning centre run by the John Clare Trust. Two mile south of the village is one his favourite places, the Swaddywell Pit Nature Reserve (TF 118029), which he knew as "Swordy Well" and which was the inspiration for his poem railing against the hated Enclosure Acts of the time:

> *There was a time my bit of ground*
> *Made freemen of the slave*
> *The ass no pindar'd dare to pound*
> *When I his supper gave*
> *The gipsy's camp was not afraid*
> *I made his dwelling free*
> *Till vile enclosure came and made*
> *A parish slave of me*

Thirty years after Clare's death, L. P. (Leslie Poles) Hartley (1895-1972) was born in Whittlesey, the son of a Peterborough solicitor. In 1908, the family to moved to Fletton Towers in Queens Walk (TL 190976). He was sent to boarding school, becoming head boy at Harrow public school before studying modern history at Balliol College, Oxford. After writing a several short stories, his first full-length novel, *The Shrimp and the Anemone*, was published in 1944. *The Brickfield* (1964) was set locally. He was awarded a CBE in 1956 for his contribution to literature.

His best-known work is *The Go-Between* (1953), which was made into a 1970 film, with a star cast that included Julie Christie and Alan Bates, in an adaptation by Harold Pinter. Although Hartley later lived a nomadic existence, travelling around the world, he often returned to the family home in Fletton, where his younger sister Norah lived until her death in 1994. It is now a private residence. Hartley was a member of the literary aristocracy.

He was a close friend of Aldous Huxley and for many years was the lover of Lord David Cecil. But he became increasingly troubled in his later years and died an alcoholic.

His life was very different to his contemporary, H. E. (Herbert Ernest) Bates (1905-1972), who was born a few miles up the River Nene, in an ordinary red brick terrace house at 51 Grove Road, Rushden (there's a blue plaque on the wall to mark his birthplace). There is also a road named after him to the west of the town.

Bates was the son of a director at a local shoe factory and attended Kettering Grammar School, which he left at the age of 16 to become a reporter on the local newspaper, the *Northampton Chronicle & Echo* (where, by coincidence, I was to work too, more than half a century later). But he didn't enjoy the drudgery of life as a junior newshound and left to work in a warehouse, writing short stories in his spare time. He was just 20 years old when his first novel, *The Two Sisters*, was published.

A prolific writer, H. E. Bates averaged a novel and collection of short stories every year for the rest of his life. Of these, his most famous creation was the Larkin family, who appeared in the novels *The Darling Buds of May* (1958), *A Breath of French Air* (1959), *When the Green Woods Laugh* (1960), *Oh! To Be in England* (1963) and *A Little of What You Fancy* (1970). Nearly two decades after his death, they were adapted for television as *The Darling Buds of May* ITV series, which featured "Pop" Larkin (David Jason), "Ma" Larkin (Pam Ferris), Mariette (Catherine Zeta-Jones), and Cedric "Charley" Charlton (Philip Franks), and topped the ratings in the early 1990s. His earlier novel *Love for Lydia* (1952) was also adapted for television in the 1970s. Its setting was inspired by Rushden Hall (SP 955660), which today is the headquarters of the town council and open to the public.

Many of his books feature local places, including *The Feast of July* (1954), which traces the journey of a pregnant young woman along the River Nene from Wisbech to Wellingborough. His 1937 travelogue, *Down The River*, describes a boat trip along the Nene near Oundle, in which he describes the hump-backed bridge at Lilford (TL026837) as "the finest in all England".

During World War II, H. E. Bates was commissioned into the RAF to write morale-boosting stories about the people fighting it. They were published under the pseudonym of "Flying Officer X" and were published in book form as *The Greatest People in the World* and *How Sleep the Brave*.

Meanwhile, Lotte Kramer had a very different sort of war. Born in Germany in 1923, she lived in the town of Mainz until 1939 when her Jewish family, fearful of the Nazis, put her on one of the last Kindertransport trains to Britain. She later found they had all perished in the evil death camps.

Lotte moved to Peterborough in 1970 and began writing poetry in 1979. Today she still live sin the city, in Longthorpe, and is regarded as one of the world's finest Holocaust poets, although her work is also inspired by the fenland landscape around her adopted home. Back in 2008, she told Nene Valley Living that one of her favourite places is Orton Lock on the River Nene (TL 166971), which reminds her of the River Rhine of her childhood.

Another living writer is Edward Storey, who was born in Church Street, Whittlesey, in 1930. He too was inspired by the flat landscape around his home town and his first volume of poetry, *North Bank Night*, was published in 1969. The North Bank of the Nene (TL 254987) runs alongside the river to the east of Peterborough and from there you can see the broad sweep of the flat, almost treeless landscape, with Whittlesey's brick chimneys smoking in the background.

Edward's recollections of his childhood, growing up in the brick town, appear in *Fen Boy First* (1994). He has written 14 books in all – all with a strong local affinity.

He says that among his most inspirational places locally are Woodwalton Fen (TL 234848), near Ramsey, Welney Wildfowl Trust reserve (TL 545946), Crowland Abbey (TF 242102) and historic Fotheringhay (TL 061929).

These days, Edward lives in Discoed in Powys, Mid Wales. He moved there in 1999, after many years living in Peterborough Cathedral Precincts – which is where this story begun. We've now come full circle in our literary tour, but I doubt if this is the end of the story. I'm sure Peterborough and the Nene valley will inspire generations of writers to come.

The John Clare Trust: http: www.clarecottage.org
H. E. Bates fans' website: www.thevanishedworld.co.uk

Walking in BB's footsteps

Entering the sleepy village of Sudborough from the A6116, the first house you see is a distinctive former toll house, known as the Round House. It was once the home of one of Britain's greatest children's authors, who wrote under the pen-name 'BB'.

His best-known book was *The Little Grey Men*, published in 1942, which won him the prestigious Carnegie Medal for children's literature in the same year. It was about the last gnomes in England and was among 20 children's books he wrote and illustrated, although he signed his illustrations with his real name, Denys Watkins-Pitchford.

His other children's books included *Brendon Chase* (1944), about two young brothers who run away from home to live in the woods – a ripping adventure yarn that has delighted generations of youngsters, myself included. That alone would be enough of a legacy for most writers, yet 'BB''s list of achievements goes way beyond writing books for children. He was also a talented artist, inspirational fisherman, one of the country's best-loved wildfowlers and a spearhead of the butterfly conservation movement. And, better still, he was a local man – and you can visit many of the places that inspired his writings.

Denys Watkins-Pitchford was born in 1905 at Lamport, near Northampton, the son of the local rector. As a boy he loved to wander the fields and brooks, and it was during his early years that he insists he once came across real gnomes by a local stream. They would later be his inspiration for *The Little Grey Men*.

As 'BB' grew older, he began to draw and write about what he saw. He eventually studied at the Royal College of Art and in 1930 became an art master at Rugby School. His first book, *Wild Lone*, the story of a fox, was published in 1938. At the same time, he penned a weekly column in the *Shooting Times*, which he was to continue writing for half a century (His pen-name 'BB' came from a size of lead shot). Also a keen angler, in 1950 he wrote *Confessions of a Carp Fisher*, which was the catalyst for a new movement in the world of angling. Before his book, nobody fished for carp because they were considered "uncatchable"; today the carp is Britain's most popular fish.

'BB' married his wife Angela in 1939 and the couple had two children, although one died at age of seven. Angela died in 1974, but 'BB' carried on living at the Round House, which was just a short walk from Fermyn Woods. Dismayed at the decline in butterflies due to the use of pesticides, 'BB' made it his personal mission to reintroduce the magnificent Purple Emperor butterfly to Fermyn, by collecting the eggs and hatching them at home in special breeding cages. His efforts were so successful that Fermyn Woods have since become the Purple Emperor's greatest stronghold in the UK and every June and July hundreds of butterfly fans from all over the country flock there to see these remarkable insects.

The local countryside was always his inspiration. In 1967 he wrote *A Summer on the Nene* about a boat trip on his local river and his 1961 book *The Badgers of Bearshanks* was based upon the real wood of the same name, near Lyveden New Bield. Close to his former cottage runs a tributary of the Nene, Harper's Brook, about which he wrote: "Standing on the old stone bridge the other day and looking over at the brown stream where the minnow shoals were spawning, I began to think about this little stream, how it has run down the centuries way back into the mists of time. Trees die, as does all life, but this bright water runs eternally, truly as old as the hills."

'BB' was awarded the MBE for his services to children's literature in 1990. He collapsed and died the same year, aged 85, but his legacy lives on, including 59 books illustrated with his distinctive scraperboard images... and those Purple Emperor butterflies, of course.

The BB Trail: From 'BB''s former home the Round House at Sudborough (OS map reference SP 971 821) there is a public footpath that crossed the A6116 to Fermyn Woods.

The best time to spot Purple Emperor butterflies is late June and the best places are at SP 966 855 and SP 975 840. Bearshanks Wood (SP 998 858) is best approached from Pilton, or by foot from Lyveden New Bield (SP 983 854). To stand where 'BB' stood to watch Harper's Brook flow under the stone bridge, go to Sudborough (SP 965 820).

What the Dickens...

February 7th 2012 would have been the 200th birthday of Charles Dickens, the writer who lifted the lid on Victorian society and gave us classic novels like *David Copperfield, Oliver Twist* and *Great Expectations*. The rash of costume dramas on TV to mark the occasion hardly did the great man justice.

Dickens' novels and short stories are populated with astonishingly-lifelike pen portraits of the people of his day – rich and poor, heroes and villains. And they still come alive today, leaping from the page to pull you into the Victorian world that he described so vividly that it has come to be known as Dickensian.

To achieve that, he was a keen observer of people. And he travelled the length of the country to watch them and entertain them in equal measure. He was a frequent visitor to this area, giving several lecture tours... and even writing about the poor catering at Peterborough Station. Some things never change...

"Charles Dickens visited Peterborough on a number of occasions and seems to have made an impression on us one way or another!" says Stuart Orme, of Peterborough Museum. "In 1837 he is reputed to have visited Peterborough and gone to the old workhouse on Westgate (today the Wortley Almshouses pub). These are said to have informed his description of the workhouse in Oliver Twist, and the character of Mr Bumble was based on the Peterborough Beadle."

It is also suggested by many experts that Dickens did the very first of his famed public readings in Peterborough in the autumn of 1852 (although Chatham in Kent stakes the same claim). But he definitely did visit the city to do some of his famous readings, on December 18th, 1855. Says Stuart: "In 1856 he changed trains at Peterborough North railway station (the modern station site), where he went to the station cafe. He got appalling service, 'a bun of great antiquity' and 'sat meekly in the cafe, my tears merging with the tea...' He wrote an ironic piece for a magazine on the experience."

Dickens came back for more readings on October 19th, 1859, reading scenes from *The Pickwick Papers* and *The Story of Little Dombey*. The *Peterborough Advertiser* described the event in glowing terms, paying tribute to Dickens' "essentially dramatic genius", adding: "This appears not only in his works but in his success as an actor, and anyone who has had the good fortune to listen to one of his speeches will be ready to admit that here as well as elsewhere the same power is exhibited.
"His voice, manners and features are each in their several ways instruments for the manifestation of his power, and when, as in the reading of his own works, its very highest pitch of development is reached what wonder that the effect is great, and that our emotions seem to be at the command of a potent magician, who, at will shakes us with laughter or moves us to tears!"

Dickens was also delighted with this reading, writing in a letter of the Peterborough event that "We had a splendid rush last night; I think the finest I have ever read to... It was as fine an instance of thorough absorption in a fiction as any of us are likely to see again."

The local Dickens connections don't end in Peterborough. The writer was a big friend of the Watson family, who lived at Rockingham Castle, and spent many summers there. Rockingham was described in *Bleak House* and he dedicated one of his most acclaimed novels, *David Copperfield*, to Richard and Lavinia Watson. During one stay at Rockingham, he claimed to see the ghost of a woman roaming the gardens. He is also known to have stayed at the Saracen's Head Hotel, in Towcester, which features in Dickens' first novel, *The Pickwick Papers*.

Charles Dickens was born in Portsmouth, on February 7th, 1812, and died in Higham, Kent, on June 9th, 1870. He was buried at Poet's Corner, Westminster Abbey. He was married to Catherine. They had ten children. His novels included: *The Old Curiosity Shop, Oliver Twist, Nicholas Nickleby, Barnaby Rudge, A Christmas Carol, Martin Chuzzlewit, A Tale of Two Cities, David Copperfield, Great Expectations, Bleak House, Little Dorrit, Hard Times, Our Mutual Friend, The Pickwick Papers.* He also wrote for several magazines and in 1836 edited *Bentley's Miscellany*, a popular magazine of the time.

The Editor with ink in his veins

Mike Colton swept into Peterborough in 1969 as the brash young editor of the *Peterborough Standard*. He stayed at the helm until 1985. Now in his 80s, and widowed with two grown-up children, he has lived in Nassington for over 40 years. And he still has strong views on the place he calls home, as I found out when he allowed me to fire the questions...

How did it all start?
By accident! I went to school at Long Eaton, near Derby, and loved reading. I decided to become a journalist and joined the *Leicester Mercury* as a reporter. A few years later I applied for a job as editor of the Maidenhead Advertiser and got it. It was the perfect job, but one day in 1968 I was walking to work and thought: "I've got another 30 years of this. Maybe there's something else to be done".

I decided to take on a new challenge while I was still young enough. I saw an advert for an editor of a new newspaper that was starting up in mid-Wales, applied for the job and got it. I handed in my notice and my wife Jean and I held a wild party to celebrate. Clearing up mess the next morning, the phone rang and I was told the paper had folded and there wasn't a job after all. I was on the dole... an out-of-work editor.

Luckily, I managed to talk myself into a job as a sub-editor on the *Guardian*, because the bloke who interviewed me shared my interest in the life of Lord Nelson. Then, a year later, I saw the job advertised for editor of the *Peterborough Standard*, applied for it and got it.

Describe Peterborough in 1969...

It was an exciting place to be at the time, which is why I went for the job. The Peterborough Development Corporation had been set up and what was a small provincial town with a cathedral was set to grow at an astonishing rate. At the time, there were three newspapers in the town – the *Evening Telegraph*, the *Peterborough Advertiser* and the *Peterborough Standard*. The challenge was to increase the circulation.

Did you succeed?

The growth in population never produced the circulation we expected, but we had a lot of fun trying and produced some great newspapers along the way.

Was the Peterborough Development Corporation a good thing?

It was social engineering on a huge scale. I remember going to the opening of new housing development in Bretton back in the 1970s and noticing how small the windows were. I was told it was because the houses were built so close together and the windows were small so the neighbours couldn't look in. It was down to finances – they had to tighten the ship and they did it by squeezing in more houses.

But at the same time, the PDC did some wonderful things. Ferry Meadows is something to be proud of – so is the two golf courses in the city. I wish they'd built a decent concert hall, but I'm glad they didn't build a university. There are too many of those in the country already.

Looking back, what were the biggest successes and failure of Peterborough's growth years?

I thought Queensgate was magic. That whole area before then was back streets and alleyways. It looked dreadful – there's no doubt about it. But it's a great shame that the big High Street names moved in and there was no room for the little shops.

And the worst?

The walkway – the footbridge – near Peter Brotherhoods. It looks like a drunken spider. I also think they should have moved the market back to Cathedral Square, where it used to be. It would have brought the city centre to life.

Meanwhile, how was the newspaper going?
We had some terrific fights with the *Evening Telegraph*. They were trying to emulate the national tabloids by calling themselves the 'Tingling ET', while we were a weekly newspaper concentrating on the hard news and the issues that affected local people. When I came here in 1969, the proprietor said the *Peterborough Standard* was the third newspaper in the city. During my time as editor it overtook the *Peterborough Advertiser* to become the second best-seller after the evening paper.

I had a terrific staff. My junior reporters included Richard Littlejohn, who is now a star columnist on the *Daily Mail*. He had great promise, but he got into a few scrapes. One day I sent him out to do a story on football hooligans and somehow he got into a fight and ended up in court. Very embarrassing. Another reporter went on to become political editor of the *Sunday Times*; another became editorial director of Westminster Press. I was very proud of them all.

What advice do you have for today's young journalists?
It's the best job in the world: enjoy it and tell the truth.

Is the truth the most important thing?
I never believed in campaigns or investigative journalism – just the hard facts. That's what people want to read.

So is that what a good local newspaper's all about?
Exactly. A local paper should be like a town getting to know itself. It's like two people leaning on the garden gate and chatting about what's going on. From an editor's point of view, it's about being on the side of the underdogs – the little old ladies. Local papers can work wonders for them.

Give us an example...
One cold winter many years ago when I was on the *Maidenhead Advertiser*, the local gas board cut off the supply when they were changing to natural gas. The little old ladies of the town were literally freezing. I contacted the chairman of the gas board to investigate and he swore he didn't know what was going on. But supplies were restored the same day.

Have you made any mistakes?

One of our reporters once drove past a house covered in placards. It turned out that the person who lived there was in dispute over ownership. We ran the story, then we found out that it was a family row and that an injunction had been served. A judge read the story and decided that we could be in contempt of court. I could have gone to prison! But we held our nerve and said: "We'll see you in court". Then they backed off. I wrote a personal letter about the situation to Harold Evans, who was then editor of the *Sunday Times*. To my horror, he published it! Luckily I didn't go to Pentonville. A few months later, I went to a conference of editors and Harold Evans was the guest speaker. He stood up and said: "I'm going to make a speech today about my old friend, Mike Colton...". My fellow editors were very impressed!

As an editor, I would have been prepared to go to prison. But I would have preferred not to. I'd rather go across the road to the Black Horse for a pint...

Who has most impressed you over the years?

The ordinary people. The humble men. I was particularly impressed by those who fought in the second world war. Some years ago I met a veteran of the D-Day landings in 1944. His name was Douglas. He'd never been back, so I took him across to Normandy on the ferry from Portsmouth to the place where he sheltered from the shells raining down on him. He described it, we found it, but he said he couldn't be sure it was the exact spot. He was a real hero, but he didn't want a fuss. He died three or four years ago.

And the least?

The politicians and bigwigs of this world. They don't deserve the praise. It's the Douglases of this world who deserve it.

What newspapers do you read?

The *Daily Mail* and the *Evening Telegraph*. I also listen to Radio 4, but I'm fed up with the political correctness. It's one of the evils of modern society. It blinds us to the truth: it stops us from discussing the issues we should be talking about.

Like what?

Immigration, for example. Back in the early 1970s I served on the Race Relations Council in Peterborough, and I was very enthusiastic, but things haven't turned out as we expected. Multiculturalism isn't a good thing, but integration is. Multiculturalism has divided the country, but integration would sort things out within a generation. Also, I hate minor politicians interfering in my life. When I started as a reporter, local councils cleared the rubbish and kept the roads clean. Now they want to prosecute me for putting out the wrong sort of rubbish. They don't bother to consult the voters any more.

Any other pet hates?

Yes – unpunctuality. The other day I went to the dentist and the receptionist said: "We're running 20 minutes late. I hope you don't mind." Well, I do. And I told her so.

Do you have any hobbies?

Absolutely none. Someone once told me that being an editor was my hobby and he was probably right. The only hobby I have these days is clearing out the shed.

Do you support Peterborough United?

I'm not a football fan, but I'm always pleased to see Posh do well.

Do you have a favourite restaurant?

I live opposite the Black Horse and I go there twice a week. It's been here since 1674, so it must be doing something right...

Do you like Peterborough?

I like Peterborough because I have so many fond memories of the city. But the city centre has become a dirty place and needs cleaning up. Some of the estates leave a lot to be desired, and I think life must be pretty miserable for some of the people who live there.

If you could live your life again, would you change anything?

I'd still be a journalist, but I'd organise my career differently. I'd go to university first and then work on a daily newspaper. But there's not much I would have changed. I've had a wonderful life.

Chapter 4

Brewing up a storm

For many people, happiness means a pint of real ale. And if you're one of them, Paul Hook has probably made you very happy indeed, for this is the man who brought you Charters (the floating pub by Peterborough's town bridge), the Brewery Tap (the city's first brew pub) and the award-winning Oakham Ales brewery.

Today, Oakham Ales is one of the best-known small breweries in the country, thanks to its fine brews like the legendary JHB (Jeffrey Hudson Bitter), which was crowned Champion Beer of Britain in 2001. "JHB certainly put us on the map," says Paul.

But a lot of water has flowed down the Nene past Charters in the decade since then. When Oakham Ales was founded in 1994, it brewed ten barrels of beer a week. These days, it produces up to 500 barrels a week and employs 20 people. What is the secret of this local success story?

It all started on the River Nene in 1985 when Paul set up the Key Ferry boat service from Peterborough's Embankment, taking parties along the river to Ferry Meadows or the Dog in a Doublet sluice. "That's how I got into the hospitality industry," recalls Paul. "Then over a pint one night I had a great idea – why not get a bigger boat, permanently moored, from which I could sell food and drink..."

In 1990, after six weeks on the continent, searching for the right vessel, in Holland Paul found the Leendert-R, a big Dutch barge built in 1907 for carrying grain and coal along the River Rhine. Although it was built for inland waterways, he sailed it across the North Sea to the estuary of the River Nene at Sutton Bridge and steered the 176ft vessel upstream to Peterborough and its final resting place by the town bridge. The first job was to empty 150 tons of sand from the barge's holds, which had acted as ballast for the sea journey. "It went to create the bunkers on Thorney golf course," says Paul.

When Charter's opened to the public in 1991, there were eight real ales on tap. Says Paul: "I'd told my bank manager that it would take four months to get the business up and running, but within three days we were mobbed and that's how it stayed. It seems Peterborough's drinkers wanted real ale too."

By 1994, among the ales sold at Charters were beers from a new micro-brewery, Oakham Ales, which had been founded in Rutland by another real ale fan, John Wood. "He used to deliver our barrels from the back of his Citroen estate car," recalls Paul. "He was a lovely man who made lovely beer."

A few years later, when Paul and his business partner John Bryan decided to open a brew pub in Peterborough's former employment exchange at 80 Westgate, they invited John Wood to join the business, but instead he decided to sell Oakham Ales to them. The Brewery Tap opened in 1998, with brewing going on behind a huge glass wall facing the public bar.

"We thought we had the capacity there for a long time to come. It was much larger than the old premises in Rutland, but soon demand was outstripping supply," says Paul.

This success was in large part due to the company's innovative approach to brewing. Exciting new yeast varieties were imported from the USA and Oakham Ales became famous for a new generation of light, zesty beers that were far removed from many of the heavy, malty brews of yesteryear – and encouraged a new generation of beer drinkers raised on lager to switch to real ales.

This approach was epitomised by the legendary JHB, which won awards at beer festivals all over the country – including of course the biggest award of all, Champion Beer of Britain, in 2001. It was named after the pint-sized Jeffrey Hudson, an 18-inch-tall man who was born in Oakham in 1619 and became court jester to the ill-fated King Charles I.

After the king lost the English Civil War, Hudson fled to France with the king's widow, Queen Henrietta Maria, but was expelled from her court when he killed a man in a duel! He was later captured and enslaved by pirates before returning to England, where he died in 1682.

When the Brewery Tap was threatened with demolition to make way for the new North Westgate development, Paul and John decided to move production in 2006 to a new brewery at Maxwell Road, Woodston. These days, Oakham Ales produces five permanent ales – JHB, Inferno, Citra, White Dwarf and Bishop's Farewell – the latter named after the much-missed former Bishop of Peterborough, Bill Westwood. There are also seasonal and special brews, some of which are exclusive to the 200 pubs that have become members of the "Oakademy of Excellence" which, as Paul explains, is bestowed upon inns that serve Oakham Ales to perfection.

Today, the company is a far cry from its early beginnings. Two years ago, Adrian Posnett was appointed managing director to bring his sales and marketing expertise to the business, and demand has continued to grow at between 25 to 30 per cent, every year. The company recently doubled the size of its Woodston site by taking on the empty warehouse next door.

But there is no danger of Oakham Ales becoming a brewing giant and losing its identity, as Paul explains: "We are still a tiddler. We make as much beer in a year as Carlsberg waste when they clean their tanks! We have got great products and, with the help of our team, are getting them into the market place, with new products coming through all the time. Every day here is very exciting. But above all, I would like to stress that Oakham Ales' success has been down to a passionate team of people who have been with us from the word go."

Designer Cider

Cider has come full circle. What was once a rural cottage industry lost to the big brewers has now been reclaimed by country folk, with a host of artisan ciders now available across the UK. And one of the latest to join the ranks of designer ciders is local producer Jollydale.

The business of turning fermented apples into a refreshing alcoholic beverage was once known to all country folk as the best way of using up windfall apples. Every cottage had its own apple tree, so every cottager has his or her own recipe.

It remained a cottage industry until the last century, when the big brewers muscled in. At the same time as real ales were being replaced by wishy-washy keg beers, traditional ciders were being usurped by bland, pasteurised versions. But while the powerful CAMRA (Campaign for Real Ales) protest movement rescued real ales from oblivion, real cider didn't have enough allies to enjoy a similar comeback.

For decades, cider had a bad press. It was the cheapest booze on the supermarket shelves, much beloved by teenagers who wanted to get drunk quickly and cheaply. Real cider was all but forgotten apart from diehards in the south-west who stuck by their beloved "scrumpy" recipes. Cider was distinctly unfashionable – until a decade ago when it suddenly became trendy... thanks to Ireland, of all places. Over the last three decades I have spent a lot of time in Ireland – much of it in the nation's celebrated bars – and cannot remember ever seeing an Irishman partaking of a pint of cider. Then Magners came along.

Brilliant marketing saw Magners Irish Cider become the drink of choice for young people. This renaissance for cider eventually saw more adventurous drinkers eager to sample ciders for themselves – preferably from smaller cider-makers.

Around the same time – 2005, to be exact – local businessman Simon Dale began experimenting with the surplus of apples from the 15 trees in his own garden at Woodnewton. He bought a press to extract the juice, fermented it and bottled 20 gallons of the resultant brew. "I'm not a cider drinker, but it did taste good," recalls Simon. "Not that I tasted much of it – my children and their university friends consumed the lot that first summer!"

All considered it a great success and Simon continued making cider – each year producing more and more until 2009 when the bold decision was made to go into commercial production.

That year, 50 tons of apples imported from Shropshire were minced, pressed, fermented and bottled to produce 30,000 litres. Although Simon's home at the Old Mill, Woodnewton, remains the hub of the business, much of Jollydale's production is now carried out in Stamford, where for the last 35 years Simon has run the Pegasus horseshoes company.

Jollydale currently produces four bottled ciders: medium sweet, medium dry and dry sparkling, plus dry still. They have been a big hit in dozens of local pubs. Simon plans to expand the range by brewing a perry beverage from pears, plus non-alcoholic apple juice. If business continues to boom, he may even consider brewing a draught version of his cider. "The future does look bright," says Simon. "Ciders seem to be here to stay."

As an avid cider drinker myself, I must say that the dry sparkling version is my favourite, served chilled. It's almost up there with my personal favourite, Aspalls (against which all other ciders should be judged, in my opinion). I would certainly encourage locals to give Jollydale a try... but drink it in moderation – at 6% abv it's very strong!

Footnote: Jollydale cider is the ultimate eco-friendly alcoholic drink. Not only does it use unwanted apples, even its waste by-product – 25 tons of crushed apple pulp – come in useful, helping to feed a herd of 500 beef cattle in Titchmarsh. "The farmer tells me they love it, but he can't give them too much because they end up drunk," says Simon.

Hopping mad

Small is king when it comes to beer. British drinkers love real ale – particularly when it is produced the old-fashioned way, by small local breweries. It is all a far cry from the 1960s and 70s when the big breweries like Watneys tried to foist bland, fizzy keg beers upon us. The drinkers wouldn't have it; they set up a hugely-successful pressure group -Camra (the Campaign for Real Ales), they voted with their feet – and they won.

Today, Watneys is no more, but small breweries are thriving. And there are none smaller than the Barrowden Brewing Company, which is run by one man, working one day a week, to supply the beer for just one pub. That man is Martin Allsopp and the pub is the Exeter Arms at Barrowden. And it's well worth a visit, because it is the only place where you get the chance to sample Martin's award-winning beers.

Every Monday, Martin gets down to the serious business of brewing the 600 pints of beer that he will need to satisfy the thirsts of his eager customers over the coming week. They are all brewed in a converted barn at the back of the 17th century pub.

Martin uses only traditional ingredients – namely water, malted barley, yeast and hops. It's the latter that gives beers their sharp, distinctive flavour and Martin actually grows some of his own hops against the warm, south-facing stone wall of the barn. He uses them in his Own Gear beer, which won first prize for the Best Bitter at the Leicester Beer festival in 2007. That, along with his best-selling Beech ale (a light session beer), Hop Gear (a strong bitter) and Black Five (a dark porter) have seen him pick up the prestigious Spring Pub of the Year award this year by the Rutland branch of Camra.

With such accolades, you'd expect Martin to cash in on the demand and sell his ales to other pubs, but he refuses to do so. "I brew my beers for my own pub," he explains. "They are unique to the Exeter Arms and have helped me carve out my own niche in these difficult times, when a lot of village pubs are closing. We are well supported by the locals as well as drinkers who come from further afield to sample my beers. I don't want people going to other pubs to drink them!"

The Exeter Arms is Martin's first pub. Until he took it on, he had worked as transport manager for a major health food chain based in Leicester. "It's been hard work – Sharon and I work 80 hours a week and haven't had a holiday in five years – but we wanted a challenge... and we got it!"

While Martin brews the beer and runs the bar, Sharon runs the 40-seat restaurant and the B&B accommodation.

The menu boasts traditional, home-cooked pub grub at sensible prices and has already won them a listing in the Michelin Guide. The pub's grassy beer garden, which is about three-quarters of an acre in size, has also won them a mention in the *Sunday Times*.

The Exeter Arms is at 28 Main St, Barrowden LE15 8EQ. Tel: 01572 747247.

Farmer Fred's liquid harvest

It was a thirsty night at the local pub for farmer Fred Roughton. From the crack of dawn to nightfall he'd been harvesting wheat – a hot and dusty job that warranted a few pints of real ale before closing time…

"I must admit I ended up drinking a bit more than I should," recalls Fred. "I somehow got talking to a bloke who used to run a small brewery. He told me he'd still got all the equipment – and I found myself agreeing to buy it off him. It seemed like a good idea at the time! The next morning he rang to ask me if I was sober and whether I was serious about buying it. I had a bit of a sore head, but I said I'd come round to have a look. He took me to an old shipping container, in which he'd stored all the stuff in five years before. It had been there so long, the doors had jammed and we had to force them open.

"When we did get the doors open, a load of old barrels rolled out. I thought to myself, what am I letting myself in for? But once we'd climbed over the barrels and I saw all that lovely brewery equipment, I knew I'd have to have it. There and then I decided to build a brewery. As a farmer I had been thinking about diversifying and this was the ideal opportunity."

That was over ten years ago. Then, as now, farmers were at the mercy of supermarket chains and European bureaucrats. Many had gone bust, sold up and moved off the land. But Fred, who tills 550 acres in Northamptonshire, didn't get bitter. He decided to brew it instead.

Two of his friends, Mike Cohrs and Paul Waring, agreed to join him as business partners. Like Fred, neither had brewed beer before. Mike was a landscape gardener and Paul a former gamekeeper. But the trio of real ale fans appreciated a good pint – and they were determined to make a success of their new venture, with a mixture of enthusiasm and hard graft. They called the brewery Digfield Ales, after an old field name on Fred's farm.

Fred converted an old milking parlour on the farm into a micro brewery... and crossed his fingers. "We were worried," he admits. "There are a lot of small breweries that brew some great beer. We had a few sleepless nights wondering whether we could compete."

But they needn't have worried. Fred loaded up his pick-up truck and delivered the first brew – a 10-gallon barrel of beer – to his local pub, the Montagu Arms, in Barnwell. The next morning, the landlord rang him and asked for another: the pub's thirsty but discerning regulars had polished off the whole barrel the previous night and demanded more! As word spread through the area, more pubs placed their orders for Barnwell Bitter, as the brew had by then been christened. Drinkers couldn't get enough of it. Soon, brew maestro Mike was burning the midnight oil concocting new recipes. And, just like the original, they sold out as quickly as they were made.

"We were amazed," says Mike. "We thought we'd start out slowly and gradually build up the business as people got to hear of our beer, but the reaction was beyond our wildest dreams."

But was it just a case of loyal local drinkers supporting a local brewer? Would drinkers from further afield appreciate it? There was only one way to find out. The annual Peterborough Beer Festival, held every summer in the nearby cathedral city, is the second-biggest event of its kind in the country. The ambitious trio decided to enter three ales at the 2006 festival, to compete head to head against hundreds of fellow brewers from all over the UK and abroad. At the festival, Digfield Ales made history. The three beers they entered won two silver medals and a bronze. It was the first time any brewery had ever achieved such a feat, but since then their brews have won more awards, including gold medals.

But how did they achieve such fame, so quickly? What's the secret? Fred, Mike and Paul showed me round the small brewery and explained the process. Water heated in a giant vessel in the roof is sprayed over a tank of malted barley below and the resulting liquid is then boiled in another massive container, where hops are added, in three stages. It's then pumped into fermenting vats, where the starches and sugars are converted to alcohol for a couple of days, before the ale is siphoned off into casks. It's then left to stand for a few days – known as conditioning – before it departs for local pubs.

It sounds simple, but the character, taste, aroma, colour and strength of the beer depend on the types and quantities of malt, hops and yeast used. And with an almost infinite variety of these ingredients, plus the distinctive taste of the local water, every brew is unique. But the attention to detail at Digfield Ales means there is consistency, which customers appreciate. After all, a drinker who has a preference for Barnwell Bitter expects today's pint to taste just like yesterday's.

Digfield produces a brew for every taste. The original Barnwell Bitter has a strong, amber colour and a dry, malty taste. It is of medium strength (4% ABV). Shacklebush, at 4.5%, is a little stronger, darker and maltier. It won the gold medal at the Peterborough Beer Festival two years running, in 2007 and 2008. Fool's Nook (3.8%) is a light straw colour with a flavour and aroma bursting with hops, while Mad Monk (4.8%) is dark in colour and the strongest of the lot.

Throughout the pubs of the River Nene valley, the beers from Digwell Ales have proved to be a huge success – but that is proving to be a mixed blessing for the three men that run it. At present they produce about 45 kegs of beer a week, and the absolute maximum capacity of the converted cowshed is about 60 kegs. But the way the beers are taking off means the brewery will soon be unable to cope with demand. Then what?

"I don't know what to do," admits Fred. "It's been great fun so far – like a hobby that's turned into a business – but I don't know if I'd enjoy it as much if we were to expand. We don't have a computer. Everything is still done the old-fashioned way, on paper. If we decide to expand the business, we'll have to be a lot more professional."

Fred is also still a busy arable farmer, growing mainly wheat and rape. But he says he isn't tempted to try growing his own malting barley or hops. "I'll leave that to the experts!" he laughs.

Visiting Fred, Mike, Paul and their brewery is like turning back the clock. Or turning full circle, to be exact. Fred's family have been farming this valley for generations and there's no doubt that a century or so ago there would have been a brewery at the farm. Every farmer's wife used to brew ale for the thirsty workers. She'd bring jugs of it down to the fields, along with home-baked bread and the farm's own cheese, as lunch for the men. Back in the 1960s and 70s, it seemed that small breweries and their distinctive local ales would die. But nostalgia has beaten progress, for once. And it's thanks to enthusiasts like Fred, Mike and Paul.

At the time of writing this book, Fred has been suffering ill health and has taken a back seat in the business, which is being driven forward by Mike and Paul, who are in the process of moving to bigger premises, near Lilford. I wish them well – and Fred a speedy recovery.

Signs of the times

The Nene Valley is blessed with lovely old pubs. But have you ever wondered how they got their names? Some go back hundreds of years and have fascinating stories behind them. In this part of the world, kings, queens, landed gentry and some eccentric locals all played a part in the images that now adorn the swinging signs. Here are just a few of my favourites…

The King's Head, Wadenhoe: Although the sign depicts King Charles I, it's unlikely that my local pub, which dates back to the early 17th Century, was always so named. Why? Because Roundhead troops from the king's arch-enemy, Oliver Cromwell, were billeted here prior to the Battle of Naseby, in 1645. The Royalists got well and truly walloped at Naseby, which was the beginning of the end for the hapless Charles I, who lost the English Civil War and was eventually executed in 1649.Happily, the King's Head is still going strong after all these years. Its picturesque setting beside the River Nene makes it a popular destination.

The Shuckburgh Arms, Stoke Doyle and Southwick: There are two pubs in England named the Shuckburgh Arms – and they're situated only four miles apart, on either side of Oundle. Both are named after the Rev John Shuckburgh, who in 1818 left his huge estate in the area to the Capron family, who lived in Southwick Manor.

The Stoke Doyle Shuckburgh is a 17th Century former coaching inn, situated close to a tiny brook that's a tributary of the Nene, and has a great reputation for excellent dining at sensible prices. Meanwhile, the equally venerable Southwick Shuckburgh is one of the best real ale houses in the area and regularly features live music.

The Montagu Arms, Barnwell: There's a private room at this old stone-built pub which was reserved for when Royalty popped in for a pint. Until 1995, the next-door neighbours were the Duke and Duchess of Gloucester. The pub is named after Sir Edward Montagu, an eminent judge and politician who was granted Barnwell Manor by King Henry VIII in 1540. The Manor was bought in 1938 by the Duke of Gloucester, youngest son of King George V, with the bulk of his legacy from the late king. The Gloucesters moved to Kensington Palace more than ten years ago.

The Chequered Skipper, Ashton: There aren't many pubs named after butterflies, but this one is even rarer because it's named after a woodland butterfly that became extinct in England in 1976.

A renowned naturalist, the late Miriam Rothschild, attempted to reintroduce the butterfly to nearby Ashton Wold. She was also a world authority on fleas and played both cricket and squash for England. The village green outside the pub was for many years the setting for the annual World Conker Championships.

The Falcon, Fotheringhay: Unlike most of the historic village of Fotheringhay, the Falcon is much younger – built in the 18th Century. But in a village steeped in so much blood, it's no surprise that it boasts the ghost of a woman who has been startling staff for generations.

The former Fotheringhay Castle was the birthplace of King Richard III in 1452 and the scene of the execution of Mary Queen of Scots in 1587. At the centre of Rockingham Forest, it was a favourite hunting ground for kings and queens, who were experts in falconry – hence the name of this renowned gastro-pub.

The Red Lion, Warmington: This stone-built inn shares the commonest pub name in Britain. Why are there so many Red Lions? Because it was part of the heraldic symbol of King James I, who on succeeding to the English throne in 1603 decreed that the country's alehouses should be so named! James (also King James VI of Scotland) was the son of the unfortunate Mary Queen of Scots. Local legend has it that he ordered the demolition of nearby Fotheringhay Castle, where she was executed.

The Black Horse, Elton: Those who got drunk and disorderly in this old alehouse back in the 19th Century soon sobered up when the landlord threw them into a cell and locked them behind bars. Two hundred years ago, the Black Horse also doubled as the village gaol. And if you dropped dead at the bar? No problem. It was also the village morgue. Although it's lost those aspects of its history, the modern Black Horse is full of original beams and old-fashioned charm.

The Queen's Head, Nassington: There are a lot of pubs called the Queen's Head. But they're mainly named after the queens Victoria, Elizabeth I or Anne. But the head on this sign is that of Mary Queen of Scots. Local legend has it that the pub got its name after a macabre incident. After her execution at nearby Fotheringhay, the queen's beheaded body is said to have been transported by cart for burial at Peterborough Cathedral. But on its way through Nassington, the cart hit a pothole and the monarch's head rolled down the street... coming to a stop outside the pub. It's a tale that sounds all more plausible after a few drinks inside the modern-day pub.

The Paper Mills, Wansford: This pub is named after the former paper mills which stood nearby, utilising the waters of the River Nene for power. The mills flourished in the 18th and 19th Century, as the increasingly literate population demanded newspapers.

One mill supplied paper to the nearby *Stamford Mercury*, which was founded in 1695 and is the oldest newspaper in Britain. It also made newsprint for *The Times*. Famous former employees included William Stroudley, who later became a railway engineer at Peterborough and invented, among other things, the communication cord.

The Haycock, Wansford: This former coaching inn on the old Great North Road is named after a drunken peasant, Barnaby, who at the time of the Great Plague fell into a drunken slumber on a haycock by the River Nene, only to be washed downstream by a sudden flood in the night. He awoke the next morning, still atop of the haycock, but wedged tight against the arches of Wansford Bridge.

Thinking that he may have been swept out to sea, Barnaby asked the assembled crowd where he was. On being told "Wansford" he replied: "What... Wansford in England?" That's how the inn - and the village - got their names. Guests here have included Queen Victoria, Diana Princess of Wales and the notorious highwayman, Dick Turpin.
These are just a few of our fascinating local pubs, of course. I apologise to those I haven't mentioned and I hope that readers will support them. These days our pubs are under increasing pressure and closing at an alarming rate. I have no hesitation in blaming our useless, overpaid politicians, who allow supermarkets to sell cheap booze yet make it impossible for pub landlords to do the same.

These days you don't have to be a drinker to enjoy our pubs. Most serve excellent food, soft drinks, tea and real coffee. They are part of our heritage and long may they remain so!

I particularly love the distinctive old names of these pubs and I urge customers to protest noisily if any new marketing broom attempts to sweep away the historic name of your pub and rename it the Slug and Lettuce, or something similar. To my mind, old pub names should have protected listed status, just like the buildings themselves.

Chapter 5

The Natural World

Sometimes, the best things in life are so obvious that you don't even notice them. And in that category I would place the wonderful, unspoilt woodlands that are right on our doorstep. Here in the Nene valley we may not have the dramatic scenery of the more rugged parts of the British Isles, but we do have some of the best woods.

Most of them are very old and were once part of Rockingham Forest, an ancient hunting ground for kings and queens in the Middle Ages. Today they include important habitats for rare birds, mammals, insects and plants. But most of all they are timeless landscapes where you can escape from the stresses of modern life and simply enjoy nature.

Sadly, however, they are under-used, particularly by the younger generation. But before us oldies start moaning about the youngsters of today who would rather play computer games than enjoy the great outdoors, perhaps we should wonder who is really to blame...

Scientists say the British countryside is out of bounds to today's children because their parents don't want them to get dirty. Research by Hertfordshire University revealed that middle class mothers wouldn't let their children play outdoors in case they got lost, hurt or muddy. "There seems to be an obsession about cleanliness," said Debbie Hougie, senior lecturer in rural geography at the university. "Perhaps because children wear expensive clothes, mud seems to be abhorrent."

Experts agree that children need to have adventures and take a few risks if they are to grow up as healthy, well-balanced individuals. So, are you guilty of molly-coddling your offspring? If so, why not go down to the local woods and see what's on offer? A good place to start is at Fineshade Wood, where the Forestry Commission and the Royal Society for the Protection of Birds share a purpose-built visitors' centre, complete with car parking, café, toilets and shop.

From here, paths radiate out into the forest for walkers, runners and cyclists of all ages and abilities. There is also a regular programme of organised events and walks for parents and toddlers.

For wildlife fans, this is the spiritual home of one of the conservation movement's greatest success stories in recent years – the re-introduction of the endangered red kite. In just two decades, a bird that had been virtually extinct in lowland England for more than a century has thrived to the extent that there are now over 500 of this magnificent bird of prey living locally. It is very rare day that you visit Fineshade Wood without seeing several – sometimes dozens – of red kites soaring above the tree tops. And even if you are unlucky, the RSPB has set up a live nest cam so that you can watch the young chicks being raised.

Another wood with excellent public access is Fermyn Wood, with ample parking and visitor facilities at Brigstock Country Park. Here there is an adventure playground for the kids, as well as all-weather paths through the trees that offer easy access for the elderly, disabled and parents with pushchairs. The wildlife speciality at Fermyn is the rare Purple Emperor butterfly that can be seen high in the branches of the wood's ancient oak trees during sunny summer days. (It also has questionable feeding habits – it can sometimes be seen on the forest floor, when it comes down to feed on deer poo.)

In early summer, large numbers of Painted Lady butterflies often appear, blown across from the continent. They appear to find our woods to their liking as they feed on the nectar of the wayside flowers. The magnificent Silver Washed Fritillary is also common here.

At all the woods you are likely to encounter deer if you walk quietly at dawn and dusk, when these shy creatures come out of the dense undergrowth to feed in the grassy rides. The fallow deer tend to travel in family groups, while the smaller muntjac are usually solitary.

In fact sunrise and sunset are the best times to see most woodland wildlife. If you're lucky - and very quiet – you may witness a fox stalking a rabbit to provide breakfast for its hungry family of cubs.

At least once or twice a week I walk the quieter public footpaths around Fermyn Wood and Lyveden – and although I encounter (and photograph) plenty of wildlife, it is rare to meet another human in that wonderful hour first thing in the morning when you have this magical landscape all to yourself.

Other woodland highlights locally include Short Wood (access off the Oundle-Southwick road), which is a mass of bluebells between the end of April and May, and Glapthorn Cow Pasture (between Glapthorn and Upper Benefield) where the blackthorn thickets host nesting nightingales. The best time to listen to their unmistakable singing is as dusk falls on a warm evening in late spring when the males are calling for mates.

Back at Fineshade, rangers to organise events to appeal to all age groups. Children are especially well catered for, and the woods are a popular destination for school parties. There is a craft fayre at Top Lodge the first Saturday of every month, plus regular walks and tours for all age groups. Log on to the website www.forestry.gov.uk/toplodge for further details, phone 01780 444920 or email: northants@forestry.gsi.gov.uk.

The visitor centre at Top Lodge, Fineshade Wood, is signposted off the A43 between Stamford and Corby. Fermyn Woods are situated off the A6116 Corby-Thrapston Road, near Brigstock.

Safari on your doorstep

There have been deer around here for a very long time. Soon after William the Conqueror's success in the Battle of Hastings in 1066, he created a royal hunting park. It was known as Rockingham Forest and covered most of the north-east of Northamptonshire, between the rivers Nene and Welland. Today, much of the forest remains – and so do the deer.

It is claimed that Britain's deer population is at an all-time high. That may come as a bit of surprise to many people who have never seen a wild deer, but there are a couple of reasons for that:

Firstly, the people who make this claim this are invariably the people who have a vested interest in the lucrative business of killing them.

Secondly, deer are, of necessity, shy, retiring creatures that rarely venture out from dense cover except in early morning and late evening. They have developed this habit because some humans like to kill them.

To see deer, you need to get up early – before dawn, in fact. You then need to be quietly in place at the edge of a woodland ride or clearing before the family groups venture out to feed, or you may see them in open country as the family groups migrate from one wood to another. But once the sun has risen above the horizon you're unlikely to see anything at all.

The red deer is the UK's biggest native mammal. Close behind it is the fallow deer which, along with the much smaller muntjac, are the commonest species to be found in this area.

Their presence in our woods is a thorny subject. Traditionally, foresters have mixed feelings about deer. They say that deer can cause damage to young trees by nibbling on the bark and young shoots, yet they bring in lucrative income from the shooting fraternity eager to get Bambi in their sights. As usual in the UK, there's a compromise. Deer are tolerated in limited numbers... and shooting enthusiasts pay for the 'privilege' of keeping those numbers down.

Deer are shy and retiring because centuries of hunting have made it a necessity. After all, their survival largely depends upon them keeping out of the way of mankind. In economic terms that's a shame, because the deer of our local woods would be a much more valuable asset alive than dead. Instead of a handful of hunters, Rockingham Forest could attract thousands of families eager to enjoy the sight of our biggest native wildlife in its natural environment. And if that sounds unlikely to you, compare it to the modern safari businesses in southern and east Africa, which in the early years of the last century were the exclusive preserve of big game hunters. Today, big game are protected and millions of tourists fly in, with their cameras (and credit cards) at the ready.

And it's a camera I use, of course, to capture these wonderful creatures. I have photographed lions, elephants, giraffe, hippos, crocodiles and rhinos in the wild in southern Africa, but I get every bit as big a thrill when a family of fallow deer appears in my viewfinder in Fermyn Woods.

Modern digital technology has made top-quality cameras more affordable and a simple DSLR with a powerful telephoto lens is all that's needed (that and the ability to get up very early in the morning!).

It is my hope that one day the people entrusted with running our woodlands will allow our native wildlife to enjoy the same respect and protection we now afford the fauna of Africa – and that our local woodlands will become the happy hunting grounds of people wishing to sample the simple delight of watching our gentle native deer unmolested in their natural habitat. You can but dream.

Welcome to the great outdoors

Everyone has their heroes and one of mine is bushcraft guru, Ray Mears. So a few years ago, when I got the chance to interview him, I was thrilled. We arranged to meet in a car park near his home in rural Surrey. It was a very windy day, but Ray turned up on time, in his Land Rover. As he opened the driver's door, a gust of wind caught a McDonalds wrapper from inside his vehicle and blew it across the car park. "I was late back from London last night and hadn't eaten," explained a red-faced Ray. But I didn't mind: Ray obviously didn't get to be the shape he was by restricting his nibbling to roots and shoots.

But the truth is, I envy blokes like Ray, who make their living from by perpetuating the wilderness survival skills of our ancestors. There's even one who lives locally…

If you go down to the woods today, you could learn a thing or two. Especially if the woods are near Wansford and survival expert Andrew Shaw is in residence. Andrew, from Peterborough, runs Fragile Earth – a company that specialises in teaching bushcraft to modern folk who have never had to forage for food or sleep under the stars.

He is a tutor of Stone Age skills to pupils of the i-pod generation and his classroom is the great outdoors – a secret private wood, deep in the countryside, where everybody gets the chance to live like their aboriginal ancestors.

Adults can live for a day or two like TV's Ray Mears. But it's even better for children, who are able to discover what it's like to be kids again – climbing trees and getting dirty in a safe environment (just like they used to before adult spoilsports took away the fun of childhood in the name of over-zealous Health and Safety).

In many ways it's the kids that benefit most, as Andrew's outdoor workshops lure youngsters away from the games console and telly. Many schools in the area send groups of children to Fragile Earth, knowing that bushcraft combines elements of maths, geography and science. The kids are getting educated, but having so much fun they don't notice. But the fun isn't just for children. Adults love getting back to basics – searching for wild food and then cooking it over a camp fire they've built from wood they've collected themselves and lit with a spark and tinder. You even get to eat your hard-won meal with a spoon you've carved yourself... from a branch that only minutes before was growing on a tree.

And it's then you realise that the simple pleasures in life are often the most satisfying. Wealth and rank counts for nothing in the woods. Surviving in the wilderness is the greatest leveller of all.

Fragile Earth offers a variety of courses, ranging from one-day bushcraft basics to weekends under the stars. You can forage for wild food and find delicious wild mushrooms. The courses are suitable for all ages. Full details on the website: www.fragilearth.co.uk

Lament for Whittlesey Mere

Whittlesey Mere was a wonder of the watery world. Situated on the edge of the Fens close to Yaxley, Farcet, Holme and Stilton, it was once England's largest lake south of Windermere.

Its size varied according to the season. About three and half miles east to west and about two and a half miles north to south in summer, it could swell to twice that area in winter. The old course of the River Nene flowed through the middle of it.

Two centuries ago, on the low ground that exists a mile or so south-east of Yaxley village, there was an inland port where fenland lighters – the barges that were the heavy haulage vehicles of their day - docked to unload their cargoes on the banks of this inland sea.

Back then, Whittlesey Mere was inhabited by a hardy breed of men and women who led a tough existence, catching fish and shooting and trapping wildfowl from its windswept waters. Known as the Fen Tigers, they were feared for their prowess in bare-knuckle fighting and admired for their mastery of skating. The hard winters of the 17th, 18th and 19th centuries turned the mere into a huge sheet of ice for weeks on end, where the population of Peterborough and miles beyond would descend to enjoy the greatest natural playground of its kind.

Big prizes were on offer for the speed-skating championships, which thousands would attend, and the top skaters of the day could cover a mile in three minutes as they skimmed effortlessly across the ice. In the summer, it became a pleasure boater's playground and huge regattas were held there. The aristocrats of the day decamped to Whittlesey Mere for weeks on end, most notably in 1774 when George Walpole, third Earl of Orford, sailed an armada of nine boats carrying his cronies and long-term mistress to the mere for a month of frolics.

But the greatest asset of Whittlesey Mere was its wildlife. Numbers of ducks, geese and waders were estimated in the hundreds of thousands and they shared the shallow water and its vast reedbeds with the secretive but plentiful bittern, a member of the heron family. It's now extinct in the Fens, along with the once-common Swallowtail and Large Copper butterflies and countless thousands of less colourful species of flora and fauna.

They're extinct because Whittlesey Mere, and the unique habitat it provided for them, no longer exists. In the late 1840s, a group of venture capitalists got together and decided they could make a quick buck by converting the watery paradise into lucrative agricultural land. This, remember, was in the days when wealthy landowners could do more or less whatever they wanted.

They first tried to drain the mere by gravity – cutting ditches and drains and hoping the water would seep away of its own accord – but although they succeeded in reducing the size of the lake, the land remained waterlogged.

Their scheme was eventually made possible by the invention of the Appold centrifugal pump, by the engineer John Appold. He'd designed it principally for draining coal mines, but its sheer power – it could shift almost 70 tons of water a minute – meant it attracted rave reviews at the Great Exhibition held in the Crystal Palace at London's Hyde Park in the summer of 1851.

The men who plotted to drain the mere, led by wealthy Holme landowner, William Wells, bought an Appold pump four feet in diameter, powered by a 25-horsepower Amos and Easton steam engine, and installed the new equipment in a brick-built building in the south-east corner of the mere (Ordnance Survey ref: TL 237 903). They also dug a new drain to take the water to the nearby Bevill's Leam drain, close to the hamlet of Pond's Bridge (known these days as Pondersbridge).

Within weeks the mere was dry, leaving millions of unfortunate fish to gasp their last on the mud left behind. Among them was the greatest pike ever reported from the British Isles – a monster reputed to weigh 52 lb. The wildfowl and rich insect life, of course, had long since departed.

As the last of the mere's waters ebbed away into the Bevill's Leam and hence through the Middle Level system and out to sea, Wells and his friends held an extravagant champagne-fuelled party at the pumping station. These rich men knew that by destroying this watery paradise they were going to get even richer.

They were proved right. Before drainage, the rental value of Whittlesey Mere (as a fishery) had been just £30 a year. The marshland that surrounded it was useful only for cutting reeds for thatching and could be rented for between one and two shillings (5p to 10p) an acre. After drainage, as prime agricultural land, this same ground was worth £40 an acre.

Wells celebrated by building the Admiral Wells pub at nearby Holme, named after one of his illustrious ancestors. It was – and still is – the lowest pub in the British Isles. This part of the world is largely at or below sea level. If the sea was to break through during at the height of a high spring tide in The Wash, this place would be 16 feet or more below the waves. But don't let that put you off drinking there. The Admiral Wells is famous for its range of real ales and well worth a visit – if only to say that although you've visited some low pubs in your time, but this is the lowest of them all... (TL 197 876)

Once Whittlesey Mere was drained dry, finds on its newly-revealed bed included the fossilised skeleton of a killer whale, a prehistoric dugout canoe preserved in the peat, and treasures from nearby Ramsey Abbey that included a silver censer and incense boat that were made about 1325 and later lost overboard, most likely when monks were fleeing the abbey at the time of the dissolution of the monasteries in 1539. They are now on display in the Victoria and Albert Museum, London.

Meanwhile, the low-lying ground that was once the bed of Whittlesey Mere was about to get even lower as the saturated peat dried out and shrank. Once dry and exposed to the air, it was attacked by bacteria that literally devoured the rich organic matter. Much of what was left was often blown away by the winds that raked across this open, flat landscape.

To measure the rate of shrinkage, Wells had a great iron post sunk deep down into the soft peat at Holme Fen so that its top ended up level with the surrounding soil surface. Within ten years, the top of the post protruded six feet above the ground; by 1870 it was nine feet.

Since then, the shrinkage has slowed down, but erosion of the dry topsoil means more peat is disappearing every year and the post currently stands more than 13 feet above ground level. The Holme Fen Post, and a 1963 replica built alongside it, stand in what is now the Holme Fen Nature Reserve and are Grade 2 listed 'buildings'. To see them, take the road from Yaxley to Holme and turn left about half a mile before Holme. They are on the right after the level crossing (TL 204 893).

Before the drainage of Whittlesey Mere, this part of the world was several feet above mean (average) sea level. It is now several feet below. This shrinkage of the peat means that the cost of keeping it drained gets greater every year, as the massive electric pumps employed today have to literally pump the floodwater uphill to take it away. With the land getting lower and sea levels getting higher, there will clearly come a time when it is no longer economically viable to keep much of the Fens drained. There are many that say that point has already arrived and that the true extortionate cost of perpetrating the 150-year-old folly of Wells and his cohorts into modern times is disguised by the various generous subsidies that exist for drainage of agricultural land.

The draining of Whittlesey Mere is perhaps typical of much of the vandalism the Victorians inflicted on the natural world, but it in no way diminishes the tragedy of the act that wiped out an invaluable natural resource as well as a way of life.

The year 1851 sounds a long time ago, but it isn't really. I put it into perspective when I remind myself that old men I knew as a child would have known old men who knew Whittlesey Mere. For example, my maternal grandfather, George Banyard, was born in 1890. At that time the mere had only been drained 39 years. Grandad grew up in an isolated cottage at Cock Fen, near Welney, and from an early age – probably 13 or less – George worked as a reed-cutter and thatcher in the Fens. As a young man he would no doubt have worked alongside older men who could recall Whittlesey Mere in all its glory. Unfortunately, Grandad George died in 1959, when I was just three years old. He must have heard some amazing tales of the old Fens. How I wish he'd lived long enough to tell me them.

Past generations certainly had mixed feelings about the drainage of the Fens. Some were happy to see the back of the mosquito-infested swamps that caused them misery through flooding and malaria. Others, whose living depended upon catching fish and fowl and cutting reeds, were outraged. They distrusted the ruling classes with a passion that extended to their choice of religion, too.

Nonconformist chapels sprung up in every Fen village, where lay preachers would often rage against the ill-advised drainage schemes. They meant, of course, that Man shouldn't rule over Nature, nor God's Will. They predicted great floods and loss of life for tampering with the natural order. They had a point: they certainly had a better perception of the inherent dangers in unthinking drainage than the profiteers.

Happily, today we stand a chance of seeing a return to the Fens of old. Ironically, it's very much down to money again – only this time it is large sums of money being invested to reverse the mistakes of the past. The Great Fen Project is an innovative scheme that will eventually see more than 7,000 acres of farmland in the Whittlesey Mere area restored to natural fenland. That's an area bigger than the original mere and its surrounding wetlands.

The project is a joint venture by conservationists and local authorities, which seeks to buy back agricultural land, field by field, acre by acre, until it can restore this remarkable corner of our region to its original, wild, fenland state. The aim is to connect the nature reserve at Holme Fen to that of Woodwalton Fen (TL 234 878), about two miles to the south by purchasing the agricultural land in between and returning it to its pristine, pre-1850 status.

By creating a larger reserve like this, it will be possible to encourage the return of rare species of flora and fauna that fail to exist in a smaller pocket of suitable habitat. For example, previous attempts to re-introduce the Large Copper butterfly have failed because the area they were released in was too compact to provide a home diverse enough for them to flourish. The Great Fen Project could see large coppers, swallowtails, bitterns and huge pike returning to these parts.

Ironically, the Great Fen Project involves pumping the contents of the Victorian water courses that were dug to drain Whittlesey Mere back onto the fenland nature reserves to keep them wet! This truly is a case of history turning full circle. The Great Fen Project is only the start of something far bigger, One day, even the dimmest of our poorly-illuminated politicians will realise that the value of undrained and wildlife-rich fenland is far more valuable in terms of tourism, education and general leisure than it ever could be as agricultural land, given the fact that it costs so much to preserve its artificial status quo.

There will come a time, as sea levels relentlessly rise, and the general population realises the importance of conservation, that more of the Fens will be restored to their original state. Indeed, if those who predict the consequences of global warming are right, the waters will one day be lapping at Peterborough's doorstep.

In 1997, when I wrote the first edition of my book *The River Nene from Source to Sea*, I argued that Whittlesey Mere would one day return whether we like it or not... and that we might as well embrace the idea and allow it to happen sooner rather than later.

I was born in the Fens long after they were drained, yet the romantic in me longs for a return to a watery wilderness that neither my late grandfather nor I ever knew – and I can only dream of. Meanwhile, the realist in me shouts that a natural fenland would earn many more tourist dollars than the sterile fields propped up by artificial drainage. I do hope that it happens in my lifetime. If only it had never happened at all. The Great Fen Project will return a huge swathe of the Fens to their natural undrained state.

Postscript to the Great Fen Project

I wrote the above words in 2006. Just a couple of years later, I was able to tell a different story...

Did you know that you're living on the edge of the most exciting conservation programme in Britain? If not, the odds are that you haven't heard about the Great Fen project. And if you haven't, you soon will.

The Great Fen project is currently recreating part of the wetland wonderland that was once the Fens of East Anglia. It is 10,000 acres in size. And if you're not sure how big that is, it's roughly the area of greater Peterborough.

Next time you take the train from Peterborough to London, look out of the window on the left-hand side between Yaxley and Huntingdon and try to imagine all those flat fields transformed into a unique nature reserve. If your imagination fails you, don't worry: the reality is just around the corner.

Just imagine: a huge, glorious wilderness of mysterious pools, whispering reedbeds, wild flower meadows and leafy glades, which you can share with hundreds of species of rare birds, mammals, amphibians and plants. And right on your doorstep. Excuse my generous use of superlatives, but this huge labyrinth of wetland trails truly puts the maze into amazing.

It is backed by a formidable array of heavyweight figures, both political and cultural. Its patrons include the Prince of Wales, former PM John Major, broadcaster Stephen Fry and Baroness Barbara Young. Backers include local councils and national conservation organisations and – most crucially – the Heritage Lottery Fund. It is huge grants from the latter that have speeded up a process that had been expected to take a lifetime of hard graft and fund-raising. Instead, it is proceeding at a dizzying pace.

But how did it all come about? To understand that, we need to look back on the history of the Fens themselves. Sitting here today in one of the driest corners of these islands, it is hard to imagine that a vast swathe of East Anglia, from Lincoln in the north to Cambridge in the south, was once a near-impenetrable morass of water, willow and reeds. Places like Peterborough, Market Deeping, Thorney, Ramsey, Crowland and Spalding were mere islands that peeped above the surrounding wetlands. But Man was determined to change the natural order of things and reclaim the wilderness to graze animals. Two thousands years ago the Romans were the first to attempt to drain the Fens, followed over the centuries by the monks from the various abbeys that were built on the islands.

In the 17th Century, Dutch drainage engineers excavated new channels to speed up the passage of the water to the sea and, in so doing, turned the natural Fens into a patchwork of summer pastures that still flooded in winter. Windmills speeded up their efforts, but it wasn't until Victorian times and the advent of the steam engine that the fully-drained fenland landscape that we know today was created.

With hindsight, it is easy to criticise the Victorians: they were arrogant enough to believe they could subdue nature and, it would appear, pretty blinkered about the consequence of their actions. William Wells, squire of the village of Holme, south of Yaxley was among them. Ironically, the new-found wealth the productive new land yielded allowed him to indulge himself and his friends with lavish shooting parties. To this end, he allowed 660 acres of his land to be left wild, to create a shooting covert. Today, that patch of land is Holme Fen National Nature Reserve.

Not all wealthy men were like Wells, of course. Step forward Charles Rothschild, a member of the fabulously wealthy banking family. Alarmed at the fast-disappearing natural fenland, along with its native species of birds, butterflies and wetland plants, in 1910 Rothschild purchased over 500 acres of undrained fenland at nearby Woodwalton for his private nature reserve. He was just in time: within a few years, 99 per cent of the original fens had disappeared. Today, his reserve is known as the Woodwalton Fen National Nature Reserve.

The object of the Great Fen Project is to connect and surround the two reserves at Holme and Woodwalton with a huge reserve – 10,000 acres – the likes of which even Rothschild could not have envisaged.

But one man who did allow himself to dream was Alan Bowley. He became warden at Woodwalton Fen 17 years ago, at a time when most of the general public saw nature reserves as somewhere pleasant to walk the dog... and anyone who proposed un-draining the fens as a bit of a nutter.

A visionary many years ahead of his time, Alan recognised the inadequacy of the fenland nature reserves at Holme and Woodwalton. They were too small to allow the survival of rare fenland butterflies like the swallowtail and large copper, due to inbreeding and the fragile nature of the small tracts of wild land, surrounded by arable fields and their accompanying cocktails of deadly pesticides and artificial fertilisers. "We always knew that we were doing no more than tending flowerpots," says Alan. "The Fens had been shattered into millions of tiny fragments. I hoped that one day we'd be able to attempt to put some of them back together. But ten years ago it seemed an impossible dream."

Although his wasn't a lone voice, he was shouted down by lots of people with vested interests and scaremongering stories to tell. Misguided, or plain mischievous, voices claimed in the local press that restoring the old fens would risk flooding local homes and cause people to die of malaria. Yet it was another scare story that caused a mood-swing among the general public and ensured that Alan's dream was shared by others. It was called global warming.

Climate change and the inherent risks of rising sea levels and flooding meant that drainage interests began to come onside. The Middle Level Commissioners, who are responsible for keeping most of the Cambridgeshire and West Norfolk Fens drained, knew that they would probably need more capacity for excess floodwater in the dark decades to come. About 10,000 acres would do nicely, so now they are among the unlikely backers of the Great Fen Project. But they are very welcome, all the same.

Sadly, the project will not see the restoration of Whittlesey Mere itself. That's out of the question because shrinkage of the peat in other parts of the surrounding fens means it is no longer the lowest part of the area. But new wetlands will be created instead, and they will be linked with the adjacent old course of the River Nene, allowing access and mooring for pleasure craft.

Access for the general public is of huge importance to the project. Without it, the scheme would never have received grants from the Heritage Lottery Fund – about £10 million so far – which enabled it to buy the surrounding fields from local farmers and landowners, plus the backing of local councils, who recognise that the Great Fen will become a huge tourist attraction, akin to the Eden Project in Cornwall.

It will certainly be a wildlife paradise. Otters have already been spotted at Woodwalton and the extremely rare bittern, a member of the heron family, is a regular winter visitor. The marsh harrier, a magnificent bird of prey, has returned here to breed. In time, the lovely swallowtail and large copper butterflies could again flit among the reedy margins. And it's all happening now.

Even in his wildest dreams, Alan hadn't expected to see the Great Fen Project completed in his lifetime. He'd always reckoned it would be a 50-year programme at the very least. But now it's all in place, he's encouraged that the public's new sympathy for all things green will see an expansion of the project. Who knows, one day it may grow to link up with the new green park pencilled in for the former brickworks around Yaxley, as well as the woodland of the fen edge to the west of the site. How long before the Fens become a National Park?

For local people that's wonderful news for both the environment and the economy, but we're still being short-changed compared to what our ancestors enjoyed before the fenland landscape was plundered by the greedy Victorians. "If the Fens had never been drained, this would now be a world heritage site every bit as important as any other wetland in the world," says Alan. "We must now try to create our own bit of rainforest in the Fens." And my guess is he'll do just that.

By a strange coincidence, I find myself writing the footnote to this story on March 16th, 2012 – exactly a century after Charles Rothschild gathered together a group of like-minded conservationists to form the Society for the Promotion of Nature Reserves (SPNR). The society was formed to identify places which needed protection and encouraged landowners and others to carry it out. Within three years, a list of 284 proposed nature reserves in the UK had been drawn up, including woods, fens, moors, meadows, downs and commons.

A century on, there are now 2,300 reserves run by the UK's 47 county wildlife trusts. And it's all thanks to Rothschild's initial success at Woodwalton Fen, where you can still visit the bungalow on stilts that he built there a century ago to live in when he made conservation history by creating his own watery wilderness.

Back from the dead: the Red Kite

Less than 40 years ago there was just a single red kite left in Britain. Today there are thousands. The spectacle of this great bird of prey soaring high above the Nene valley is an everyday sight we now take for granted. But the red kite's revival is a miracle that even the most optimistic ornithologist would never have dared dream of back in the dark days of the 1970s.

Even in these environmentally-conscious times, you're more likely to hear of an endangered species pushed to the brink of extinction than a real success story. But the dramatic comeback of this most enigmatic bird of prey is something we can all be proud of, because as little as a generation ago it simply couldn't have happened.

In medieval times, the red kite was common throughout the country, both in the countryside and in towns and cities. In fact it was awarded Royal protection in the streets of old London because its scavenging habits helped keep the streets a little less filthy. But when the capital's thoroughfares ceased to be open sewers, its importance was diminished. And when the landed gentry enclosed the countryside and instructed their gamekeepers to wage war on all birds of prey, its fate was sealed.

But it was a case of mistaken identity. The red kite doesn't kill pheasants, partridges, lambs or anything much bigger than an earthworm. It feeds on carrion – dead animals. But the fact that it had a hooked bill made it guilty as far as our hardline ancestors were concerned as they commenced to slaughter it. By 1800 it was extinct in England. By 1900 it survived only in a few isolated pockets in rural Wales. The devastating effect of the deadly pesticide DDT, which made its eggs infertile, exacerbated the bird's plight.

The red kite's nadir was reached in 1977, when only one bird – a solitary female – was recorded in Wales. Surely it was about to join the beaver, wolf, great bustard and large copper butterfly on the ever-lengthening list of species now extinct in the UK? That it didn't was thanks primarily to a far-sighted group of landowners in Wales who afforded sanctuary to the endangered bird. Soon a breeding population was re-established and the birds began to thrive, to the extent that their sanctuary at Rhayader, Powys, became a tourist attraction.

With DDT and other noxious chemicals finally outlawed and numbers of other birds of prey like buzzards and sparrowhawks increasing again, the RSPB decided to the time was ripe to re-introduce red kites. They started in the Chilterns and Scotland. It was an immediate success and the birds soon bred and began to spread.

One particularly adventurous bird from the Chilterns broods was seen one day in the early 1990s soaring high above Fineshade Woods, near King's Cliffe. The person who spotted it was local wildlife ranger, Carl Ivens, who realised the mixture of woodland and open countryside in the area would be ideal for another re-introduction.

In 1995, in great secrecy, 25 young birds were imported from Spain, along with 25 chicks from the Chilterns nests. They were introduced to Fineshade, with the full backing of the wood's owners, the Forestry Commission. The success of the scheme surprised everybody. Today there are estimated to be about 500 birds in the area, which have naturally spread throughout the Nene valley and into the outskirts of Peterborough itself.

But the biggest stronghold is at Fineshade itself, which received a development grant of almost £1 million to convert former Grade II-listed farm buildings into a visitor centre, run jointly by the Forestry Commission and the RSPB, along with the Rockingham Forest Craft Guild. Here, you can learn about all aspects of forest life, including the rich history of the former Rockingham Forest which once covered the vast majority of this area.

But the highlight for most visitors is the chance to see red kites in the wild. Most days they can be seen soaring above the trees and, in the breeding season, a concealed nest-cam delivers live pictures of the adults feeding their hungry chicks. You can learn more about the birds from two of the full-time staff at the centre – the RSPB's Chris Andrews and Susan Taylor, of the Forestry Commission. Both are equally enthusiastic about the forest and its wildlife.

"Red kites are inoffensive birds that tend to eat only carrion," says Chris. "This area is ideal for them as it is a mixture of woodland where they can roost and nest and open countryside where they can feed. There is plenty of food for them here – much of it road-kill from the nearby A47 and A43. Red kites are not territorial like most birds of prey, so it is commonplace to see groups of them flying together. It's a magnificent sight."

It's a sight that Susan also enjoys on a daily basis. At the Top Lodge visitor centre she is helping to create a brilliant destination for families, with plenty to keep all age groups occupied and fascinated all day long. The centre is packed with informative displays about the forest, its history and its wildlife - and the old woodland crafts are not forgotten. Visitors can see the ancient practice of coppicing, charcoal burning and iron smelting. They can even buy a bag of Fineshade charcoal to take home for the barbeque!

"There's a choice of walking, riding and cycling trails through the forest, including two paths with a hard surface suitable for wheelchairs and children's buggies," says Susan. Back at the centre, there's a big adventure playground where the youngsters can let off steam while exhausted parents enjoy refreshments at the café.

Much of Fineshade Woods is ancient broadleaf woodland, more than 400 years old. In its glades live herds of fallow deer –descendants of those that were hunted by England's early kings when Rockingham was a Royal forest. But its star residents are those red kites, which are now afforded official protection.

Unfortunately, even in these more enlightened times, there are still gun-happy morons who will still shoot rare birds of prey. There have also been reports of red kites that have been deliberately poisoned. But happily, the idiots are in a minority and the area's red kites are popular with almost everyone. I say "almost" everyone, because there are one or two local residents who have suffered the embarrassment of having their underwear on display on TV thanks to these birds.

Chris Andrews explains: "Red kites like to line their twiggy nests with soft material. This usually means bits of sheeps' wool from hedges and fences, but they will also steal items from washing lines, which end up in the nests and on the nest-cam! Shakespeare wrote: 'When the red kites builds, look to your lesser linen'. So this is nothing new!"

Wild flowers

One of life's greatest joys is walking through a meadow or wood in spring, surrounded by wild flowers. Here in Northamptonshire, you don't have to go far to appreciate them: the ancient woods of Rockingham Forest and the lush, damp meadows by the River Nene are great places to appreciate our native flora, but you don't have to wander through picture-postcard countryside to enjoy wild flowers.
Some of the best are to be found in inhospitable places like wasteland and old quarries. Take the Hills and Holes, just outside the village of Barnack, near Stamford. This hummocky landscape is a former limestone quarry. It was first exploited by the Romans, more than 1,500 years ago, but excavations continued through the Middle Ages for stone to build great ecclesiastical buildings in the East of England, like the magnificent cathedrals at Peterborough and Ely.

The quarry was exhausted 600 years ago, but nature reclaimed the rubble left behind and today it is a wild flower haven of national importance, with over 300 wild plants recorded, including eight species of orchids. Throughout the summer, this 22 hectare reserve, managed by Natural England, is awash with colour from wild flowers, including some rarities.

But wherever you are, there is a real thrill when you do find a rare wild flower. Recently I chanced upon a beautiful creamy-white flower in a damp corner of a local wood. Much thumbing through the pocket guide book ensued before I identified it as an Early Marsh Orchid – the first I'd ever seen. But you don't have to identify rare species to enjoy wild flowers. The everyday and commonplace are often the most spectacular. It would be a hard-hearted person not to be moved by the sight of a carpet of Bluebells in the dappled light of a fine spring evening. Short Wood, near Oundle, is one of the best places in Northamptonshire to see Bluebells (although most of the other local woods also boast excellent displays).

I've often stood transfixed admiring vast areas of bluebells, bathed in dappled shade. At times like this you realise that no matter how hard we contrive to make our gardens look natural, it just doesn't compare to the results of the random chaos of nature's own planting schemes.
But Bluebell woods are much more than an object lesson on how to achieve naturalised gardens; they're an important indicator of the age of the wood itself.

Long-lived trees like the oak will come and go in the time it takes the Common Bluebell (Hyacinthoides non-scripta) to spread and achieve that sea of blue. Bluebells, along with other stars of the forest like Wood Anemones, Violets, Primroses, Ramsons (wild garlic) and Wood Sorrel are all tell-tale signs that you're most likely to be walking in ancient woodland. The more present, the more ancient it's likely to be.
It is estimated that 70 per cent of all the world's Common Bluebells are found in Britain's woodlands, but they are under threat – from unscrupulous plant rustlers and, I'm sorry to say, gardeners. The plant rustlers are the thieves who dig up bluebells and sell them to unwitting gardeners. This is strictly illegal – our native bluebell is a protected species under the Wildlife and Countryside Act 1981.

Gardeners are to blame for choosing to grow the native Bluebell's close relative, the Spanish Bluebell (Hyacinthoides hispanica) in our gardens. These escape into the wild and hybridise with native Bluebells. Like most hybrids, they show extra vigour, and there's a real risk of them running amok among our ancient woods and smothering the natives. And that would be a tragedy.

So, let's make sure we stick only to native Bluebells in our gardens… and only buy them from reputable suppliers. That way we can ensure that spring's finest natural display will be there for future generations to enjoy.

Our local woods feature many more fine species of flowers, from the beautiful Wood Anemone to the secretive, shade-loving Wild Strawberry. And be prepared for a real sensory experience if you chance upon an expanse of white-flowered Wild Garlic: there are large areas of Fermyn Woods dominated by this pungent herb, which is also known as Ramsons.

One of my favourite woodland flowers is the Ragged Robin. It's beautiful yet subtle – the sort of plant that would be welcome in any cottage garden. So many of us gardeners strive to achieve the so-called "naturalised" look in our plots, yet few of us are capable of emulating what nature can do all on its own.

The majority of Britain's ancient meadows have been destroyed by modern agricultural practices, but where they do still survive, I urge you to enjoy them. It's a liberating experience in summer to push through the waist-high grasses and flowers of a riverside meadow, surrounded by the hum of insects and enveloped in the heady aroma of Meadowsweet. If ever a wild flower lived up to its name, this is the one. The lush grasslands that border the River Nene are ideal.

The traditional country names of all our wild flowers are so evocative: Shepherd's Purse, Jack by the Hedge, Foxglove, Primrose, Meadow Cranesbill, Rosebay Willowherb, Wood Sorrell. Aren't they so much better than the tongue-twisting Latin names of plants that gardening snobs love to impress us with?

The beauty of butterflies

Nothing is more suggestive of summer than the colourful butterflies that grace our gardens, hedgerows, meadows and woods. Britain has 59 species of butterflies, ranging from the commonplace Cabbage Whites, Peacocks and Red Admirals of our gardens through to the secretive and elusive Purple Emperors and White Admirals of our woodlands.

You don't have to be an early riser to enjoy them, either: these most obliging of creatures give their best displays in the middle of hot, sunny days! There's a lot to be said for butterfly watching. Besides being beautiful on the eye, they are easier to identify than most birds. While there are scores of little brown birds that look much the same, to the frustration of the budding bird watcher, most butterflies are unmistakable.

Butterfly spotting is also ideal for youngsters. Give them a simple guide book, like the *Collins Gem Guide to Butterflies*, and let them loose to see how many they can identify. Don't encourage them to catch them, though – butterflies are declining and we should do everything we can to preserve them.

Here's just a few of what you're likely to find (and where):

Gardens: Butterflies aren't shy. They love human company, especially when we grow insect-friendly plants like Buddleia, Verbena, Lavender and Marjoram, in our gardens, where they can feast on the rich nectar. You're bound to get plenty of Peacocks and Red Admirals, as well as Small Tortoiseshells (although the latter are in worrying decline in the UK). Some summers great swarms of Painted Ladies migrate to the UK from northern Africa and Spain and these big, beautiful butterflies will jostle with the natives for a space on the Buddleia blooms!
You'll also get Commas, Cabbage Whites, Small Whites and Brimstones, as well as a few rarer visitors.

Meadows: Grassland attracts its own selection of butterflies. Ancient meadows that have not been "improved" with pesticides and fertilisers are best – and the more wild flowers the better. Expect to find a host of brown butterflies – Meadow Brown, Gatekeeper, Ringlet – as well as Common Blues and, if you're lucky, the occasional Brown Argus (a member of the blue family, even though it isn't blue!). The Nene valley is one of its strongholds in this area. Also commonplace are the skippers – the Large Skipper, Common Skipper and Essex Skipper – with the occasional Dingy Skipper putting in an appearance. If you're really lucky, you might spot a Marbled White, especially on rough grassland on limestone.

Woodland: This is the place to find some of our most beautiful and rare butterflies. The woodlands of the east midlands are the stronghold of some scarce butterflies that have died out in much of the country, like the Purple Emperor and the Black Hairstreak. Regarded by many enthusiasts as the most prized of all British butterflies, the big, dazzling Purple Emperor prefers damp woodlands with lots of sallow bushes, on which its caterpillars feed, as well as tall trees like oak and ash where the males can roost between mating. Luckily they come down to the ground occasionally on sunny days, when the startling purple iridescence of their wings can be best seen. Fermyn Woods are probably the best place in the country to see Purple Emperors, thanks to the hard work of one of our greatest writers, "BB" (see chapter 4).

The Black Hairstreak feeds on blackthorn and, again, spends most of its life high in the canopies of oak trees. It is even rarer than the Purple Emperor, but happily Glapthorn Cow Pasture, near Oundle, is one of the UK's premier spots for this butterfly, thanks to the dense areas of blackthorn scrub that its caterpillars feed upon.

Common butterflies of the woods include the Speckled Wood. Rarer, yet still found in good numbers in woodland in many parts of this region, are the White Admiral, Silver Washed Fritillary and, if you're really lucky, the Wood White.

According to Butterfly Conservation, more than 70 per cent of our butterflies are in decline, with almost half under threat of extinction. Even the once commonplace Small Tortoiseshell's numbers have fallen 68 per cent in the last decade. Butterflies are seen as important indicators of the health of our countryside: plentiful butterflies means the environment is in good shape.

Sir David Attenborough, president of Butterfly Conservation, says: "These declines can be reversed. If you change the environment to help butterflies, all sorts of other wildlife benefits too. Nature comes back to life." That means growing butterfly-friendly plants in our garden and encouraging owners of woodland to create and maintain good butterfly habitats. For more details, visit Butterfly Conservation at www.butterflyconservation.org

Mushroom hunting

September is the time when many of us succumb to that hunter-gatherer instinct and go foraging or food in the countryside. It's when you'll find whole families gathering delicious wild blackberries for jams and puddings, or sloes and elderberries for more alcoholic tipples.

Fewer go mushroom hunting, which is a surprise considering the rich variety of fungi to be found in the UK. What puts most folk off is, of course, the fact that the mushroom's close cousin – the toadstool – is often deadly poisonous.

An expert on fungi was once asked what was the difference between a toadstool and a mushroom. He replied: "A toadstool has a cap and a stem and you can't eat it; a mushroom has a cap and a stem and you can." It means you have to be very, very careful about what you pick.

Never eat any mushroom until you are 100 per cent certain of its identity. If you're going foraging you'll need a good identification book. The best is the definitive bible of fungi gathering, *Mushrooms* by Roger Phillips (no relation). It's a big book of almost 400 pages and too large to lug around the countryside, but it's essential to have at home for reference before you commit your foraged fungi to the frying pan.
There are well over 2,000 species of mushrooms and toadstools in Britain. Of these, several are delicious, many are edible but bland, many more are inedible because they taste horrible, a lot are mildly poisonous and could causes stomach upsets... and a few will make you seriously ill or even kill you.

But don't let that dire warning put you off. Some of the best mushrooms are easy to identify: like Field and Horse Mushrooms, which are found in unimproved grassy meadows – especially those fields grazed by animals. They are delicious and taste much better than shop-bought cultivated mushrooms. They can also be very impressive: Horse Mushrooms grow to the size of dinner plates and can weight almost 1 lb each. One of those makes a breakfast all on its own!

But do avoid the similar-looking Yellow Stainer mushroom, which smells like antiseptic and, as its name suggests, discolours to a metallic yellow when cut with a sharp knife. It tastes unpleasant and can cause gastric upsets. Luckily it is very easy to identify.

In the woods, the Scaly Wood Mushroom is a real treat. It is quite common locally, often growing in rings around the base of oak trees in September and October. Like most mushrooms, it tends to die off after the first frosts of winter, but nearby you'll often find groups of Wood Blewits – beautiful, blue/violet-tinted mushrooms that will often survive through to Christmas, unless we get very severe early winter weather. Their close relatives, the Field Blewits, are fairly common in this area, where local folk call them "blue legs" on account of their pale blue stems. They can't be missed: they're usually four to six inches across and grow in huge fairy rings on old pastures. They're great for mushroom soup because, unlike cultivated and field mushrooms, they stay pale off-white and don't turn the broth a dirty grey colour!

Also growing in fairy rings are the commonplace fairy ring Champignons, which are a delicious addition to any risotto, soup or pasta dish that requires mushrooms. But these lovely little mushrooms have very tough stems, which need to be snipped off with scissors or nipped through with your thumbnail as you pick them.

It used to be thought that fairy rings were formed by fungi growing in the footsteps of fairies as they danced in circles in the moonlit meadows. Sadly, the truth is less magical.

All mushrooms and toadstools are the fruiting bodies of underground organisms – vast networks of microscopic threads that are neither plant nor animal and get their nutrients by breaking down organic matter. As the underground fungus grows, it throws up its fruiting bodies around its perimeter. Some have been found up to half a mile across, which makes them the biggest living organisms in the world.

You don't have to escape to the woods or meadows to gather delicious mushrooms. Ordinary verges and footpaths are where you'll find Shaggy Inkcaps, which are delicious if you pick and eat them when they are very young and before their gills start to turn black and inky.

The biggest enemy of the mushroom gatherer is the mushroom fly, or, rather, its larvae – maggots. Always cut your pickings in half to look for the tell-tale burrows. But I can't stress too often that the most dangerous bit is taking a chance and eating something you're not sure of, which is why I'm repeating it yet again.

Of course, you don't have to eat what you find to appreciate fungi. With so many species of mushrooms and toadstools to discover, why not just go out to admire, and perhaps photograph, these colourful wonders of the autumn countryside? After all, fungi should be fun.

Chapter 6

In Times of Conflict

The church of St John the Baptist at Thorpe Achurch stands on a ridge of high ground overlooking the picturesque vale of the River Nene, which separates it from the neighbouring parish of Wadenhoe. This pastoral scene of woodland and water meadows remains largely unchanged from the days when Robert Browne was rector. But the tranquil beauty of the setting is deceptive, for Browne was among the men to blame for the greatest tragedy ever enacted on English soil – a sequence of events that would culminate in the River Nene itself running red with the blood of massacred men, women and children. Such was the horror of the English Civil War of the 1640s.

It was a war that saw brothers fighting brothers, neighbours fighting neighbours. No corner of the country was spared its horrors – and our region was at the heart of the conflict. To understand its causes, you have to go back a century to the reign of King Henry VIII and his break from the Roman Catholic Church. It left a vacuum which plenty of rival religious factions were keen to fill. Among them were the Nonconformists, who wanted a simple, pared-down church.

The nonconformist movement was founded by Browne, who was born near Stamford and was a cousin of the Cecil family from Burghley House. From 1581 onwards, he was frequently arrested for his preaching, which was declared illegal by the fledgling Church of England. He was tolerated only because of his illustrious relatives and, with their influence, became rector of Thorpe Achurch in 1591. But that didn't prevent him preaching his beliefs at unlawful gatherings and he was frequently arrested over the next 40 years.

He was finally excommunicated in 1631 and sent to prison in Northampton, where he died. But his beliefs lived on. Some of his followers left for the New World, including the famous Pilgrim Fathers who sailed from Boston on the Mayflower in 1620. Browne's son, Edward, was among the founders of Maryland.

The separatists who stayed became known as the Puritans – and among them was a certain Oliver Cromwell. He was born in Huntingdon on April 25, 1599, and educated at the town's grammar school. In 1620 he married Elizabeth Bourchier and in 1630 he moved to St Ives. At around this time, influenced by his wife's family, he became a Puritan, telling anyone who would listen that God had given him "a mission". He was also elected MP for Huntingdon.

A decade later, he had moved to Ely and became MP for Cambridge. By now he was one of the most unspoken opponents of King Charles I and the Church of England. But despite his pompous attempts to claim the moral high ground, Cromwell was – like most religious and political zealots – a disingenuous character.

He was also an early exponent of political spin. When King Charles I and assorted noblemen drew up plans to drain the fens, Cromwell won political support from the angry Fenmen by pretending to oppose the plan. Later, after the king had been deposed, he set about draining them himself.

But we're getting ahead of ourselves. Let's go back to 1639, when the king was forced to send an army to Scotland to quell a rebellion. It had been a costly business and in 1640 he summoned a Parliament to ask for funds. To his surprise, the MPs refused his demand and instead insisted on airing their grievances – which were largely religious. Angrily, Charles dissolved Parliament.

A year later, he tried again, with the same result. And this time he decided to get his way, by force if necessary, and war was declared.

London was a hotbed of Puritanism, so he headed north and formed an army, raising his standard at Nottingham in 1942. Meanwhile, the Parliamentarians gathered their own force, which were to be known as Roundheads, so called because they had short hair compared to the long, flowing locks of the more flamboyant king's men, known as Cavaliers. After a few minor skirmishes, the first major battle was at Edgehill in Warwickshire, which was a stalemate, although the Royalists had the edge.

The Parliamentarians retreated to Warwick and the king could have pressed his advantage by storming London, but he refrained from doing so – probably in the hope that a peaceful settlement was still possible. But it wasn't.

With the onset of winter, both sides took a break. Back in the 17th century, the country's primitive roads – no more than rutted tracks – became muddy and impassable. Hostilities did not resume until the spring of 1643 when the king's army stormed Lichfield and Reading. By now, the country's loyalties were divided roughly on a line from Hull to Plymouth, with the Parliamentarians to the south and east and the Royalists to the north and west. Thus Peterborough and the Nene valley was principally on the side of Parliament, yet close to the Royalist strongholds of the north and midlands.

At this stage, the king was favourite to win the war and Charles pressed home his advantage by storming Bristol, then the second city in the country and of immense strategic importance due to its port and armaments factories. But as winter again closed in, neither side appeared to have the upper hand. But as the campaign season of 1644 approached, the stalemate was broken. The 20,000-strong Scottish army marched south to join the Parliamentary army, while 5000 Irish troops joined the Royalists. Their first clash was at Marston Moor, near York, where Oliver Cromwell made an impact on the battlefield for the first time, in charge of cavalry from East Anglia. His disciplined men were instrumental in the first major defeat of the Royalists in the war. Despite this success, 1644 again ended in stalemate. The whole country was war-weary and both sides were eager for peace, yet Cromwell remained bullish. He remodelled the Parliamentary army (which hence became known as Cromwell's Model Army) and was determined to defeat the king once spring arrived.

The spring of 1645 saw the king's army storm Leicester, before heading south. The Roundheads marched north from London to intercept them. On the way, they found shelter where they could, in farm buildings and local inns. My local pub in Wadenhoe, for example, was commandeered by Parliamentary soldiers. Presumably it was some time later that it was named the King's Head! Meanwhile, the Royalists were billeted to the west of the country, around Daventry.

Eventually, on June 14th, the two sides faced each other near the village of Naseby, in the valley formed by the northern branch of the infant River Nene, close to the present A14 trunk road.

The Royalists (10,000 strong) were outnumbered by the 12,000 Roundheads, but the king's nephew, Prince Rupert of the Rhine, led a cavalry charge that saw most of the Parliamentary army fleeing for their lives. The triumphant Royal cavalry pursued them for several miles, cutting many of them down, before they set about ransacking the Roundheads' baggage train.

A couple of hours later they returned, expecting to celebrate a famous victory. But instead they arrived at a scene of bloodshed. Cromwell's more disciplined cavalry had stayed put, and the Roundhead infantry routed the king's musketeers and pikemen. Thousands of slain Royalists littered the battlefield, including at least 100 women and children who had been mercilessly hacked down by Cromwell's troops on the edge of the battlefield.

It was – and remains – the bloodiest massacre ever seen on English soil. It also spelt the end of the Civil War for Charles, who no longer had a big enough army to put up a fight. He eventually surrendered on May 6th, 1946.

The king was placed under house arrest and two years of intrigues and plotting followed, during which loyal Royalists tried to stage uprisings in various parts of the country. Meanwhile, Parliament was worried about the power wielded by the army and tried to disband it, but Cromwell would have none of it. With the backing of the militia, he insisted the king should face trial, saying: "We shall cut off the head of the king with the crown upon it".

The eventual trial was illegal. But Cromwell, now more of a power-crazy tyrant than the king had ever been, insisted it should go ahead. He even insisted that Charles was not allowed to speak in his own defence. The sham ended in the sentence Cromwell had insisted upon, with Charles indicted for treason against his people (an offence which didn't actually insist).

He was sentenced to death by beheading. Charles was executed on January 30th, 1649. In his final speech at the scaffold, the hapless king said: "I am the martyr of the people."

With the king out of the way, Cromwell snatched control. He styled himself Lord Protector, but was actually a military dictator – and an unpleasant religious zealot into the bargain.

His henchmen set about desecrating the country's churches, tearing down and destroying works of art which the bigoted Puritans reckoned amounted to idolatry. Peterborough Cathedral was no exception. The thuggish Roundheads smashed the exquisite stained glass, the statuary, carved choir stalls, the high altar and even the medieval ceiling. The cloister and Lady Chapel were also demolished.

But their beliefs didn't prevent them feathering their own nests. Cromwell's henchman, William Butler, was given funds to build a lavish town house in Oundle – Cobthorne, which still stands at 16 West Street and is today owned by Oundle School.

Life under Cromwell's rule wasn't pretty. He encouraged the persecution of witches and thousands of innocent old women were killed. Religious tolerance didn't exist, with dissenters tortured or murdered. Rebellion in Ireland was dealt with by the wholesale massacre of innocent civilians, thus sowing the seeds of discontent that would rumble on for centuries.

Cromwell died on September 3rd, 1658. He was succeeded briefly by his inadequate son, Richard, but by then the country had tasted enough of republican rule and the exiled son of the late king was restored to the throne as Charles II in May 1660. Peterborough celebrated by adding a top storey to the town hall (which still stands on Cathedral Square).

Bizarrely, in January 1661, Cromwell's body was exhumed from its resting place in Westminster Abbey, put on "trial" and hung at nearby Tyburn.

The head of the corpse was then hacked off and put on display for nearly 20 years outside Westminster Hall. It then disappeared, only to resurface as part of a gory exhibition of "curiosities" in the 18th century. In 1814, it was bought by Josiah Wilkinson and remained in the Wilkinson family until 1960, when it was presented to Cromwell's old college, Sidney Sussex College, Cambridge, where it was buried.

As for the rest of Cromwell's remains, there are rumours that the body was smuggled back to Huntingdon and buried in the town churchyard. Another legend says that devoted followers buried it deep beneath the ground at Naseby, scene of his finest hour. But the more likely explanation is that it was tossed into the common burial pit at Tyburn, London.

If you want to take your own Civil War tour of the area, why not visit the following: Thorpe Achurch (OS ref: TL 021 830), leave the A605 at Lilford; Cobthorne House, West Street, Oundle (TL 040 880), leave the A605 at Oundle roundabout; Peterborough Cathedral (TL 194 985) and the old Town Hall, in city centre; Oliver Cromwell Museum, Huntingdon (TL 241 716) is in Cromwell's old grammar school, in town centre; Oliver Cromwell House, St Mary's Street, Ely (TL 537 791), now the town's tourist information centre, close to city centre; Naseby battlefield (SP 685 799), just north of the A14. Leave at A5199 junction (and see below).

Naseby: a village in time

It's hard to believe that the picturesque village of Naseby once echoed to the sights, smells and sounds of one of the most bloody battles ever fought on English soil, but for one day in the summer of 1645 this quiet rural idyll was shattered by the decisive battle of the English Civil War.

It is said that the waters of the infant River Nene ran red with the blood spilled on the fields to the north of the village as 20,000 men fought to decide who should rule Britain – King or Parliament. By the end of the day, around 1,400 of them had been slaughtered – and King Charles I had fled for his life.

The Parliamentarians had won. Charles was executed in 1649 and Britain became a republic under Oliver Cromwell until 1660. But in Naseby, where history had been made, life went on. It wasn't until almost 200 years later that this momentous event was officially marked by a monument.

In 1823, John and Mary Fitzgerald, the Lord and Lady of the manor at Naseby, erected a gloriously over-the-top stone memorial, just outside the village, "to commemorate that great and decisive battle fought in this field", according to the inscription on the granite obelisk. Perhaps the Fitzgeralds were inspired by Cleopatra's Needle, which had been presented to Britain in 1819 by the ruler of Egypt to commemorate Nelson's victory in the Battle of the Nile over the French, who had planned to invade Egypt. They certainly weren't influenced by historical accuracy, because the bungling couple managed to build it in the wrong spot – a full mile from where the battle actually took place.
They'd mistakenly placed it on the site of an old windmill, where the Parliamentarians had grouped on the day before the battle. Their mistake was rectified a few years later when a second monument – this time a similarly incongruous stone pillar with a ball on top – was built. At least it was in the right place, on the ridge from which Cromwell's cavalry charged on that fateful morning.

It's a sobering feeling to stand at that spot, taking in the sweeping view of the rolling countryside, knowing that so many men lost their lives there in the horrific events of 1645. It is said that most of the fatalities were buried where they fell, in mass graves in those fields, although a few did get a Christian burial in Naseby churchyard. Although their graves are unmarked, another stone pillar – this time with what appears to be a Celtic cross on the top – commemorates the fallen.

A battle of a different kind was fought in Naseby 20 years ago when plans were announced to build the new A14 on a route that cut through the historic battlefield. bjectors eventually lost that fight, but the new road did bring its benefits, encouraging more people to visit sleepy Naseby and learn about its history.

Today, Naseby has its own tourist industry, complete with the Naseby Battlefield Project's own website (www.naseby.com) from which you can download a pdf map of the key locations in the battle and take part in the Naseby Battlefield Tour. It also includes the Market Harborough Civil War Trail, because the Royalist army spent the night in the nearby town before the fateful battle.

The Great War

They called it the war to end all wars. They said it would all be over by Christmas. And the young men who queued up outside the recruiting office in Peterborough's Cathedral Square believed it. Like their counterparts in every town and village across the land in the summer of 1914, they believed they were doing their patriotic duty. They saw it as a great adventure. But the great adventure turned out to be the Great War. World War I lasted four bloody years, in which 13 million lost their lives. Among them were more than a million soldiers, seamen and airmen from Britain. And among those were well over 1,000 from Peterborough alone.

It was the same story throughout the Nene valley. But while nearly every local town and village has its own memorial to its sons that lost their lives, Peterborough to its shame never bothered to erect one. It is only recently, after a passionate campaign, that local politicians finally agreed to an appropriate monument to our local heroes. Campaigners included Peterborough military historian, David Gray, who spent five years of painstaking research to unearth the stories of each and every city serviceman who died as a result of World War I.

He shared his findings in his remarkable book, *No More Strangers*, which is a meticulous account of all those tragic lives lost on the killing fields of Europe, Africa and Asia. David quotes verbatim from newspaper reports of the time, published in the *Peterborough Advertiser*, and the stiff-upper-lip language of those far-off days when the sun never set on the British Empire makes the stories all the more poignant. I challenge anyone to read it without being moved.

Says David: "The men came from all parts of the city and surrounding areas to enlist at the recruiting office, as they did in towns all over the country. The main one in Peterborough was in Cathedral Square. Men came from all walks of life and couldn't wait to join up as they thought the war would be over very quickly and they wanted to see some action.

"They often joined in groups of friends from local factories, villages, etc, and went to the same units at the front. Unfortunately this meant that they also died together in the big battles where thousands were slaughtered in a single day. The main regiment for the Peterborough area was the Northamptonshire Regiment as the city was then situated in Northamptonshire. About a third of the men enlisting in the Peterborough area went to this regiment and subsequently more local men were killed fighting in it than any other single unit.

"The men from the area fought in all corners of the world where the war was raging, including Europe (Italy, France, Belgium), the Far East, (Iraq, Palestine, Salonica), Gallipoli, Africa and even China. They fought in all the different services - Army, Navy and Air Force."

The first soldiers from the Peterborough area arrived on the western front in August 1914. The first to die was Thomas Salmon, from Eastgate, on August 26th. It was his 30th birthday.
William Wright, from Bishops Road, was due to get married in August. Instead he went to war – and died on September 25th. Charles Coyne, from Walpole Street, had been a 19-year-old butcher's apprentice in New England and was also engaged to be married. But he was fatally wounded at Ypres within weeks of arriving at the front.

The death toll mounts at every page of David's book. And in every life cut tragically short there is a sad story. Like that of soldier J.W. Sharpe, from St Margaret's Road, Old Fletton, who twice escaped death – once when a bullet passed through his haversack and again when another struck his tobacco tin – but his luck ran out when he suffered a heart attack in April 1915.

John Lee, of St Marks Street, had once been voted "Peterborough's most handsome man" in a competition at the city's Hippodrome theatre. Like many other members of the Northamptonshire Regiment, he perished during an ill-fated advance under enemy fire on May 15th. He was 37.

On May 22nd, 1915, the *Peterborough Advertiser* reported that boxing champion Robert Bull, from Wellington Street, had been killed in action. On the same day, the headmaster of St John's Boys' School in the city was informed that a former pupil and one of his teachers had been killed.

The following month, another Peterborough soldier, Henry Hatfield, of Eastgate, recovered from being wounded only to be killed in action a few weeks later. He left a widow and four young children.

Early in the war, Sergeant Tom Eustace received the DCM (Distinguished Conduct Medal) for bravery. Back home in Fletton Avenue on leave in June 1915, he'd told friends his ambition was to go one better and win the Victoria Cross. Before he got the chance, back on the battlefield on July 31st, he was gunned down.

Peterborough's first suicide victim of the war was Harold Meadows, who was found hanging from the rafters of an outhouse in Geneva Street, the day before he was due to return to his regiment. The corner's jury returned a verdict that he had taken his own life "during a fit of temporary insanity". He was 27 and was buried at Peterborough cemetery – unlike many of his fallen comrades, who was laid to rest in makeshift graves on the battlefields where they'd died.

Leading seaman Earnest Johnson, of Mayor's Walk, must have believed he had a charmed life. He survived the Battle of Helgoland and the Battle of the Falklands and two of the vessels he'd previously served in were sunk. He was in the near vicinity when the great liner Lusitania was torpedoed by a German U-boat and helped pluck victims out of the water. But he lost his life in 1916 when his final ship, HMS Invincible, didn't live up to its name. He was among the victims when it was sunk.

Corporal John Yerrell, of South Street, had died in 1915. His brother, Sergeant Samuel Yerrell, died a year later. A comrade wrote: "Poor Sam has been killed this morning... tonight I am going to see him buried respectably. First off he had both arms shattered by a bomb, and as a fellow was bringing him towards our trench, they fell exhausted. Then a lieutenant jumped out of our trench and went to help them. As soon as he got to Sam, a German fired at them, the bullet passing through Sam's neck and right through the officer's heart. The officer was killed instantly, and poor Sam died an hour afterwards before I could get to him. He died a soldier's death."

One wonders whether that was any consolation to grieving Mrs Yerrell, who had lost both her sons in the space of a year. Sadly, she wasn't the only parent to suffer a double bereavement in the tragedy. Brothers John and Harry Bright, of Fletton Avenue, both perished in France. So did Thomas and Frank Elmer, of Lincoln Road. Thankfully, Mr and Mrs Elmer's two other sons, who also served in the war, survived.

Who can imagine the heartbreak of Mrs W.C. Spreckley, of Fletton Avenue, who lost three sons in the conflict? Yet no story could have been sadder than that of Private Arthur Hogg, of Walpole Street, Peterborough, who was killed in action on May 13th, 1917, at the age of 31. By the cruellest of ironies, his widow gave birth to their only son on the same day. They had only been married 15 months. Mrs Hogg named their son after the father he'd never know.

When Robert Martin, of Belsize Avenue, Woodston, was killed in action, his commanding office wrote to his widow: "He took part with us all in the great battle of Messines and though he died his name goes down as a hero of our great Empire... although your loss is irreparable, remember he has found a great prize which all the world longs for, peace. Do try and console yourself with this thought."
Meanwhile, on August 16th that year, Frank Hendry of Church Walk was killed in action near Ypres. It was the day of his second wedding anniversary.

Not all the victims died on the battlefield. Victor Smith of Lincoln Road East, perished on October 16th when the engine of the plane he was flying stalled at 500 feet over Palestine and plummeted to the ground. He was buried at the military cemetery in Deic-el-ealah.

Elvin Watling, of Dickens Street, was reported as killed in action on November 20th – the very same day as his brother, Victor, was discharged after being severely wounded.

There were heroes a-plenty. Albert Rimes, of Broad Street, New Fletton, was killed on March 25th 1918 when he rushed out of his trench to help a wounded comrade – and was shot through the head by a German sniper.

By now the war was nearing its end – which must have been some relief for Mr and Mrs Clark of Morris Street, Peterborough, who lost their son, William, to gas poisoning. He was their third son to die... and they still had another four out in France fighting in the war.

With just a month of fighting remaining, 19-year-old Edward Crosby, of Cromwell Road, proudly arrived in France in his brand-new RAF uniform. Tragically, he was shot down behind enemy lines on his very first flight. He was buried in the nearby RAF cemetery.

The final Peterborough man to die during the conflict was Corporal William Fogarty, of Eastgate, who lost his life on Armistice Day – November 11th, 1918 – when the troop train he was travelling in derailed and crashed in France.

Every death is a tragedy, and it is a near-impossible job to sift through the stories of more than 1,000 young Peterborough men cut down in their prime to choose the saddest, yet one that tugs particularly hard on the heart strings has to be that of machine gunner Henry Hodson, of Alwalton. Before he'd left for the front, Henry had met and courted a local serving maid, who'd agreed to marry him when he was next on leave, in February 1917. Returning from the trenches, he was distressed to find that she had disappeared on the eve of the wedding.

Heartbroken, the 16-year-old soldier told his parents he was going to Peterborough to catch a train to return to his regiment. But instead he walked down to the nearby River Nene, where he left his belongings on the riverbank. They were found the next day. His body was discovered two months later, a couple of miles downstream at Orton. The coroner's jury returned a verdict of "found drowned" but few doubted that the heartbroken soldier had taken his own life.

It was not just German shells, bullets and poison gas that killed our soldiers. Disease was rife in the filthy trenches at a time when modern medicine was very much in its infancy. Nearly 150 of our war fatalities were from causes other than enemy action, with pneumonia being the biggest single killer.

How many of the survivors suffered mental health problems in the years and decades that followed? Back in the early part of the 20th century, post-traumatic stress wasn't recognised. Victim support didn't happen. Returning servicemen, however badly scarred physically and mentally, were considered to be the lucky ones. Sorrow was reserved for the fallen. Survivors were expected to get on with it.

The call to arms

World War I was triggered by the assassination on June 28th 1914 of Archduke Franz Ferdinand, heir to throne of the Austria-Hungarian empire, in Sarajevo. Austria blamed Serbia for supporting terrorists and declared war, followed quickly by Germany.

Due to complicated alliances between various European nations, other countries including France and Britain were soon dragged into the conflict, which eventually spread to other parts of the world, although the stalemate in the trenches of northern France saw the most British casualties. The first day of the Battle of the Somme on July 1st 1916 saw 54,470 British casualties. In Passchendaele, British gunners fired as many as 500,000 shells a day.

The war changed the world forever. War-weary Russians revolted in 1917, which eventually saw the fall of the Tsar and the beginning of the Soviet Union. America joined the conflict the same year.

The Secretary of State for War, Lord Kitchener, was a well-known hero of Britain's previous skirmish, the Boer War, at the turn of the century. He gained parliament's approval to raise an army of 500,000 men and allowed his own face to appear on recruiting posters. They were designed by the artist Alfred Leete, who was born in the Nene valley in the village of Thorpe Achurch, near Oundle.

Leete's "Your Country Needs You" slogan was one of the first, and most powerful , advertising messages of all time, resulting in a staggering 761,000 men volunteering in the first eight weeks of the war. I wonder how many realised what they were letting themselves in for?

Britain and France both suffered more than 1 million men killed, with the latter estimating that 27 per cent of its male population aged 18 to 27 had perished. The youngest British casualty was 14; the oldest 68. The prime of our nation's manhood had been lost.

The Dambusters' local connection

The ground shook in the darkness as the roar of heavy aircraft engines reverberated through the Northamptonshire countryside. It was March 1943 and the second world war was at its height.

Was it the Germans? Had the mighty Luftwaffe decided to home in on Corby to bomb the steelworks, or perhaps the factories of nearby Market Harborough? The ARP (Air Raid Precaution) wardens in the sleepy village of Cottingham grabbed their tin hats and gas masks and wondered whether tonight was the night when all their training would finally be put to the test.

The frowning chief warden put his forefinger to his lips and called for hush, listening intently to the sound of the low-flying bombers, getting louder and nearer. At last a relieved grin spread across his face.

"It's all right lads, they're ours," he said. And as if to confirm his pronouncement, the valley was suddenly lit up by flares dropped from the Lancaster bombers roaring across the moonlit surface of Eyebrook Reservoir.

Something was going on, but the locals didn't know what. David Dodd, a schoolboy at the time, vividly recalls looking out from his parents' cottage at Frog Island, Rockingham Road, and seeing wave after wave of heavy bombers flying low and fast across the reservoir. How was he to know that this was part of the most famous formation of military aircraft ever - 617 Squadron, led by Guy Gibson. He was witnessing the legendary Dambusters honing their skills in preparation for the most audacious aerial raid on Nazi Germany.

Back in the spring of 1943, Britain stood alone In Europe. The rest of the continent had fallen to the Nazi war machine and America had only recently entered the war. Since the embarrassing evacuation of the allied ground troops from Dunkirk in 1941, the only way to fight back was from the air. Britain wanted to slow down the relentless march of the German forces and realised that the best way to do that was to destroy, or at least badly damage, the factories along the Ruhr valley that manufactured and supplied the steel and military hardware: the tanks, aircraft, guns and shells.

Back then, aerial warfare was in its infancy and the bombardment of enemy targets was very much a hit-and-miss affair, relying upon guesswork from men working in darkness inside a plane hurtling through the sky at more than 200mph. It was inevitable that the majority of bombs missed their intended targets by more than half a mile. Hitting an armaments factory, for example, was more by luck than judgement. There had to be a better way – and that was where Barnes Wallis and Guy Gibson came in...

Wallis was the brainy inventor who realised that the best way to wreak havoc on the Ruhr valley was to attack and destroy the reservoirs that provided both water and hydro-electric power to the densely-populated area.

The only way to disable a reservoir is to bomb and destroy the stone dam that holds back the waters. But how did you accurately hit a masonry wall that is only 25 feet wide? Luckily, Wallis had devised a bouncing bomb – one that, once fired from a low-flying Lancaster bomber, would skim across the reservoir's surface and come to rest at the foot of the dam before blowing the stonework to smithereens.

But who would do it? The man for the task was Gibson – the real-life Top Gun of his day and a brave young wing commander who had already flown 170 dangerous missions over enemy territory. He was told to hand-pick his men for the top-secret assignment, known only as Operation Chastity, and thus create 617 Squadron, which would be based at Scampton, Lincolnshire.

Incredibly, Gibson and his men only had a matter of weeks before they had to put their operation into effect in May, when water levels in the reservoirs were at their highest. They urgently needed to practise and Eyebrook – built in 1940 to supply Corby steelworks – was one of three English reservoirs they used for their low-flying practise runs at just 60 feet, because it closely replicated what they would encounter for real in the Ruhr valley.

David Dodd, a Boy Scout at the time but now retired and living in Kettering, recalls: "From Frog Island we could often see Eyebrook Reservoir and aeroplanes dropping flares on it. It wasn't until later we learned that this was in fact Wing Commander Guy Gibson and his comrades practicing for the Dambuster raids over Germany."

The Mohne, Eder and Sorpe dams were the three primary targets. The Mohne and Sorpe alone held back 76 per cent of the total water available to the industrial valley. If breached, these dams would bring the whole industrial valley to a standstill, causing massive damage.

On the night of May 16th, 1943, the Dambusters headed for Germany – 133 men in 19 Lancaster bombers. In the early hours of the next morning, the Mohne, Eder and Sorpe dams were all breached, sending torrents of water 30 feet high crashing down the valley, causing immense damage. The raid caused the death of 499 Germans, 718 foreign workers and over 1000 livestock. But, more importantly, the factories, power stations and infrastructure of the Ruhr valley were crippled for weeks.

The cost to 617 Squadron was also high. Of the 19 aircraft that flew out, only 11 returned; 53 of the 133 crew were killed and three bailed out to be made prisoners of war.

Of the surviving aircrew, 33 were summoned to Buckingham Palace on June 22nd and decorated by the King, with Gibson himself receiving the highest award for gallantry, the Victoria Cross. Tragically, he returned to operations and was killed on a mission the following year. The daring Dambusters raid lifted the morale of the beleaguered British public at a time when victory against the enemy seemed nigh on impossible. It was also a huge shock to the Germans and probably helped shorten the war.

Nobody celebrated more than the folk back home in Cottingham. Because they knew.

When GIs outnumbered locals

At the outbreak of the second world war in 1939, the Nene valley had every reason to fear a foreign invasion. It eventually came in 1942 – not from Nazi Germany but from the United States of America. The mighty US Eighth Air Force came, saw and helped to conquer Hitler's evil empire. Its 350,000 airmen stationed in East Anglia also won a lot of local hearts.

Many of their airfields were clustered to the west and south of Peterborough. In the Oundle area, locals were outnumbered by the GIs stationed at Polebrook, King's Cliffe, Molesworth, Kimbolton, Glatton, Deenthorpe, Grafton Underwood, Alconbury and Chelveston. For three years, the skies were filled with heavy bombers and their fighter escorts en route for mainland Europe. Meanwhile, the local pubs were filled with thirsty airmen who, despite moaning about English beer being flat and warm, still drank plenty of it.

You can hardly blame them. They partied like it was the last party of their lives. And they knew that, for many of them, it would be. Between 1942 and 1945, 26,000 of them were killed, 1,900 seriously injured and 6,300 of their aircraft destroyed. For example, the 303rd Bomb Group – who called themselves the Hell's Angels – flew 364 missions from Molesworth, in which they dropped 26,346 tons of bombs and shot down 378 aircraft. In doing so, they lost 185 of their B-17 'Flying Fortress' bombers and 817 of their men. A further 754 were taken prisoners of war.

On a brighter note, 400 of them met and married local girls – which happened to be a record for the USAAF. Only Polebrook came close, with 250 GI brides. There's no doubt that the US airmen's success with the ladies caused a lot of friction locally – not least because many of the liaisons ended not in marriage but in illegitimate pregnancies, which in rural Britain more than 60 years ago were considered shameful. Many of the babies were given up for adoption.

The Eighth Air Force also brought a touch of Hollywood to the area. Movie stars (Major) Clark Gable and (Lt Gen) James Stewart were both based at Polebrook, the latter flying 60 combat missions in two years.

Legendary band leader (Major) Glenn Miller played his last concert for the airmen at King's Cliffe in 1944 before he died when his aircraft plunged into the English Channel en route for Paris. By coincidence, James Stewart later starred as the band leader in the 1953 blockbuster movie, The Glenn Miller Story.

The vast majority of the British population loved the Americans, of course. Until the USA entered the war, the RAF had fought a lone battle against the Luftwaffe – a battle that had strained our industrial resources and morale to the very limit. From 1942 onwards, Germany's war machine was dealt a double blow, with RAF bombers pounding the factories and cities by night and the USAAF by day.

The Americans were justly proud of their ability to pinpoint strategic targets – usually aircraft factories, oil refineries, railway marshalling yards, U-boat bases and airfields.

It was much later in the war when the Allies embarked on their controversial tactic of blanket bombing German cities – reducing historic settlements like Hamburg and Dresden to ashes and killing hundreds of thousands of civilians. But this was largely in retaliation for similar actions by Germany earlier in the war, when the bombs had rained down on Britain's towns and cities. The bombing also diverted German resources at a time when the Allies were preparing for the Normandy landings and the push into Europe that would see the end of the Nazi threat.

The Eighth Air Force left our shores in May 1945, but the legacy of their stay remains. Each of the airfields is marked by a memorial to the brave young men who lost their lives in the conflict. And although no official effort was made to preserve the buildings, many of them remain.

At Polebrook, for example, the giant aircraft hangar is now a warehousing complex, run by David Gower, whose sterling efforts to preserve what artefacts remain resulted in him being granted honorary membership of the 351st Bomb Group Association.

Much of the rest of the former airbase is on land owned by the Ashton estate and is now a nature reserve, where trees and undergrowth have reclaimed many of the old buildings and shelters. But in the remains of the crumbling old barracks there are still echoes of the airmen who lived there more than 60 years ago – including faded murals that they painted on the walls. Visiting them is a poignant reminder of the dark days and nights of the war when this corner of rural England was indeed a little America.

Where spying is an industry

Espionage. It's all 007 stuff, isn't it? Well, no, it isn't, actually. And only rarely is it about slipping deadly poison into the drink of a fellow spy. It's about intelligence gathering. And most of the folk involved in it are hard-working folk who spend the day in front of their computers. Then they go home and play with the kids.

To me, the most exciting thing about intelligence gathering is that most of it happens on our very doorstep. At RAF Molesworth, to be exact.

Molesworth is situated just off the A14. It's less than ten miles from Oundle yet it and its neighbouring base of Alconbury has a population of 6,000 (that's 1,000 more than Oundle).

It has had a colourful past. During the latter part of World War II, Molesworth was one of the most important US Eighth Air Force bomber bases.

Later, at the height of the Cold War, it was home to the controversial Cruise Missiles that could have wiped out the former Soviet Union at the press of a button or two. And with intercontinental nuclear missiles stored within its bunkers, it got the inevitable peace camps of CND protesters outside its gates.

The protestors have long gone, along with the missiles. The bunkers are empty (but still there and clearly visible from the road between Clopton and Old Weston). The barbed wire's there, too, plus armed guards and watertight security. It has to be like that, because what's going on inside is top secret.

I wanted to get inside Molesworth, but there was no chance. It's a place where journalists don't get an invite. Not because the Americans don't like us, you understand, but because things don't stay top secret if you tell everyone about them. But they were more than happy to invite me to RAF Alconbury, instead. And that's nearly as good. Perhaps I'd better explain why...

Alconbury, Molesworth and the smaller satellite base at RAF Upwood, near Ramsey, are known as the Tri-Base and are, together, home to the 423rd Air Base Group. Molesworth is where the Joint Analysis Centre is based and where all the intelligence-gathering takes place. Alconbury is where the support staff are based and where the 6,000 population come to shop, pray and play baseball. Little Upwood is where they go to the doctor or dentist.

The man in charge at the time of my visit in 2007 was Colonel Jack Jones. And he was happy to tell me about the massive operation he headed. But he was not giving any secrets away.

Col Jones ran three airbases with no planes. Not one. But he wasn't not ashamed. In fact he was very proud of the mission he was on. "Make no mistake, the mission of the Tri-Base has never been more important to what we do," he said. "You've got to realise that our mission today is very different to what it was 50 years ago. The modern air force is on the ground, in space and in cyberspace. Only a third actually involves aircraft."

And that, of course, is where Molesworth – the Joint Analysis Centre – comes in. Images from spy planes and satellites are gathered, enhanced, studied... from 91 countries in all, including Europe, Africa, Asia and the Middle East. The information is then passed on to US, Allied and NATO commanders from all military services (army, air force, navy and marines).

Of course, they don't always get it right. I'd dearly have loved to ask Col Jones about the "weapons of mass destruction" in Iraq. Was it a case of a computer operator at Molesworth getting it wrong? Or was it politicians deliberately misinterpreting the information supplied by JAC? I'd put money on the latter. But I didn't ask Col Jones, because Col Jones wouldn't tell me.

Nor would Master Sergeant Rich Romero, who was head of public affairs at the Tri-Base. But Rich did give me a guided tour of Alconbury. Here, just off the junction of the A1(M) and A14, was an amazing scaled-down version of an American town. Here was the high school... supermarket... chapel... the American football field... the nursery... the coffee shop... the internet café... the US mail post office... the fire station... the superb gymnasium complex... This was Smalltown, USA. Crime was non-existent. Everybody you meet really did say "Have a nice day". Nobody bothered to lock their cars. They didn't even take their keys out of the ignition. This is partly because the whole base was populated by decent, law-abiding citizens. It probably also had a lot to do with the fact that two police forces patrol this corner of Cambridgeshire – UK and US military police. Rich explained that anybody who strayed off the straight and narrow automatically got the toughest sentence. For example, if you were caught speeding, you would get punished by the UK or USA, whichever was the least lenient.

"In most situations, for most misdemeanours, most people would prefer to be dealt with by the British police," grinned Rich. It appeared that the military cops didn't take fools gladly. Only the young raw recruits stayed on the base, in accommodation provided. The rest lived out in the community, in the surrounding villages. Next time you drive through Sawtry, for example, look at how many cars with US number plates are parked in the drives.

Partly because of the mystery surrounding what goes on at Molesworth, there are a lot of rumours about the bases. When the very last planes – tank-busting A10 thunderbolts that served in the first Gulf War, since you ask – left Alconbury in 1995, local rumour had it that the bases would close. It's a rumour that Col Jones was quick to dismiss, pointing out that the population at the bases was actually growing, with heavy investment to match.

It's an investment that is very welcome in the surrounding area. "We make a £20 million contribution to the local community every year – and that does not include the salaries of the local people we employ on the bases," said Col Jones.

There's definitely a symbiotic relationship between the UK locals and US military personnel – and pains are taken to keep it that way. Penny Ash is a British civil servant who worked full-time here as community relations adviser. "I report to the Ministry of Defence and to the base commander. I wear two hats," she explained. "One of my jobs is to brief newcomers. I remind them that we are two nations divided by a common language.

"It is a matter of understanding and that comes through knowledge – which in itself can only happen through understanding. Community relations is a two-way street. I look at ways of integrating the two communities."

This aspect of Penny's work can range from helping a new recruit to take up a hobby outside the base to organising events in which local people can take – events that include giant hangar dances, complete with Glenn Miller-style big bands, when the guests dress up in 1940s clothes and recreate the wartime era when the giant Flying Fortresses ruled these bases.

Today's warfare – and the pursuit of peace – calls for very different weapons. The personnel based at Molesworth don't face the deadly might of Hitler's Luftwaffe on a daily basis, for the threats to world peace today come from many different sources – not the least of which is the threat of global terrorism. But their jobs are every bit as demanding.

As Thomas Jefferson said in 1801: "Eternal vigilance is the price of liberty". And at Molesworth today they are being very vigilant indeed.

Chapter 7

At work and play

Peterborough today is very different to when I first worked here, over 40 years ago. In those days the city was perennially shrouded in a haze of smoke from its belching chimneys.

Back in the 1970s, vast brickworks virtually surrounded the city. From Eye and Dogsthorpe to the north, Whittlesey to the east, Fletton and Yaxley to the south and Orton to the south-west, the horizon was dominated by the brickworks' towering chimneys, which never quite managed to take away that distinctive scent of scorched earth.

We got used to it. After all, it was a small price to pay for a vital industry that employed thousands of local people. It was the smell of success (and a darned sight less unpleasant than the sickly stink of the sugar beet factory that was situated opposite the newspaper office in Oundle Road where I started work back in 1972). A few of the brick chimneys still remain today – notably at King's Dyke, near Whittlesey – but they are a shadow of the boom days when bricks from Peterborough helped build modern Britain.

But why Peterborough? And how did it all begin? To tell that story, we need to go a long way – about 150 million years ago, to be exact, when much of what is today's Europe lied deep beneath a warm tropical sea. It was the Jurassic Age, when huge marine reptiles roamed the lush waters in search of giant squid. Ichthyosaurs and plesiosaurs swam where today we live and work. And we know that because many of their fossils have been found preserved in the sediments from the bottom of that former sea.

About 100 million years ago, the ever-moving Earth's crust began to push the ocean floor upwards, and what is now Britain began to rise from the waters, pushing that deep layer of sediment towards the surface. Today we know it as Oxford Clay. It is a relatively soft rock, but it has a very special quality: when heated, the high carbon content of Oxford clay allows it to self-ignite.

It is, literally, the clay that burns. And Peterborough just happens to lie upon a massive seam of Oxford Clay, more than 150 metres thick...

Britain has built bricks for hundreds of years, but it was traditionally done on a small, local scale. Villages had their own brickworks, where ordinary wet clay was dug from shallow pits, shaped into bricks, left to dry and then baked in small kilns. They were too heavy to be transported long distances by horse and cart, so they were used locally. But everything changed in 1880, when brothers George and Nathaniel Hempstead opened a brickworks at Fletton. They had discovered the secret of the self-firing Oxford Clay and were determined to exploit it. They dug deep pits to excavate the seams of Oxford Clay below the surface, then built special mills to grind the soft clay into a powder that could be pressed into shape. They also built special kilns that required less coal to fire the bricks – and thus kept costs down even further.

These economies of scale meant that the bricks they produced were much cheaper than those available elsewhere. Britain's newly-built railway system allowed them to send their cut-price bricks to London – then undergoing a massive building boom – and Fletton bricks became famous nationwide.

Of course, the Hempstead brothers didn't have it all their own way. Other speculators soon moved in, and land around Peterborough that contained deposits of Oxford Clay fetched high prices as new brickworks sprung up around the city, mainly close to railway lines so that it was easier to both export the finished bricks and import the coal needed to fire the kilns.

Records show that in 1898, Whittlesey Station handled 23,500 tons of incoming coal, as well as an astonishing 108,500 tons of outgoing bricks. Similar quantities were shifted from other stations, including the former Yaxley station on the Great Northern line and Eye station on the former Midland and Great Northern Joint line.

In 1899, John Hill amalgamated several of the competing brickyards to form the London Brick Company, which dominated the industry for almost a century.

At its peak, London Brick produced 2,000 million bricks a year, although its productivity was closely tied to the building industry. In the years following the second world war, as Britain strived to rebuild its bomb-ravaged cities, the brickworks couldn't keep up with demand and the company sent recruitment staff to southern Italy to encourage Italian workers to emigrate to England. About 3,000 men and 2,000 women eventually arrived in the area. Many settled and today there is a thriving Italian community in the city, particularly around Fletton.

Today, most of the brickyards in the Peterborough area have closed. The industry is but a shadow of its former self, but there are plenty of reminders of those days of scorched earth – not least the deep, abandoned quarries from which the Oxford clay was excavated. That huge lake near the Fletton Parkway is just one of them. Now filled with water, it is an attractive part of the modern city landscape... and home to a vast population of coots.

Another great scar in the ground, a former brick pit near Dogsthorpe, is now a landfill site, while the vast brickfields of Orton – all 2,500 acres of them - are midway through the 20-year process of being transformed into Peterborough's southern township. When the project is complete, Hampton should contain 7,000 homes and employ 12,000 people. The Hampton development has been constructed along sound environmental lines and part of the flooded former clay workings have been preserved and are now an important habitat for the rare great crested newt.

Over the years, the millions of tons of Oxford clay excavated from around Peterborough have revealed thousands of fossils, including some of the huge sea monsters that once swam in that Jurassic ocean, 150 million years ago. Thanks to the brick industry, Peterborough is world-famous for its fossils, many of which are on display in the city's museum.

But Peterborough brick industry's greatest legacy is the bricks themselves. It is said that more than a quarter of the current buildings in Britain were built from bricks made in the Peterborough area. Even today, ordinary building bricks are known in the trade as "flettons" – after the village where it all started, back in 1880.

Rockingham Castle's family history

Britain is famous for its castles. People come from all over the world to scramble over our monumental ruins. You pay your money and wonder what it was like, hundreds of years ago, to live in these piles of old rocks. But Rockingham Castle, just outside Corby, isn't like that. For the last 450 years it has been home to the Watson family. Before that, it belonged to the royal family. And that's quite some history.

Actually, its history dates back even further: to Iron Age Britain well before the Norman Invasion of 1066. But its prominent position, atop a high hill with commanding views across the Welland valley, ensured that King William I snatched the site and built a fortress of his own.

The Conqueror himself never visited Rockingham. But his son, William II, known as Rufus on account of his red hair, was a frequent visitor. Unlike his statesman father, Rufus was a feckless playboy who loved nothing better than hunting deer, so his forays into Rockingham Forest were frequent and he even held his councils – the forerunners of today's parliament – in Rockingham Castle. But Rufus later died in a hunting accident, accidentally struck by an arrow by a fellow hunter in Hampshire's New Forest, and gradually Rockingham lost its royal patronage. By the 15th century it had fallen into disrepair and was used only as a hunting lodge.

That should have been the end of Rockingham and, like so many other castles around the kingdom, it ought to have fallen into disrepair. But in 1485 a local entrepreneur, Edward Watson, bought the place from King Henry VIII and began a process of restoration that was to last for centuries – right up the present time, in fact.

That's because in the subsequent 450 years the Watson family has maintained Rockingham Castle as its family home. Through those four and a half centuries its future often looked in doubt – not least during the English Civil War, when it was taken by the Royalists after a suitably bloody and dramatic siege. The castle's owner at the time, Lewis Watson, was financially ruined by the Civil War, but afterwards he somehow clung on and, in the centuries that followed, the family slowly restored the place.

During Queen Victoria's reign, a regular visitor to the castle was the novelist Charles Dickens, who based Chesney Wolds in *Bleak House* on Rockingham. Today, the Saunders Watson family still live here – and welcome visitors to share their home with them. It is open regularly to the public.

Further details from the website: www.rockinghamcastle.com

The family tree

In a corner of the beautiful grounds of Rockingham Castle is an arboretum of specimen trees, including giant American redwoods that soar 50 feet or more into the sky. They've been there almost half a century, but head forester Brian Lewin knows them well – after all, he planted them.

"They were just small saplings when I planted them in 1963," recalls Brian. "I see them every day and it's been wonderful to watch them grow and mature into the magnificent trees we have today. That's what I love most about this job: being outside and working with nature, watching the seasons change and the trees growing. I wouldn't swap it for the world."

At 76, Brian is a decade past the age when most men retire, but sitting at home in front of the TV doesn't appeal. He prefers the job he has done since 1957, when he finished his National Service in the Army. It must run in the family, because Brian's father 'Winkie' Lewin was head forester before him, in 1976 receiving a medal from the Royal Forestry Society for 40 years service. Now Brian has gone one better, receiving an RFS award for 54 years' service.

And there's a third generation waiting in the wings. Brian's grandson, Gary Glover, 28, joined the estate's forestry team seven years ago.
Over the years, the Lewin family have planted tens of thousands of trees on the estate, which was once part of Rockingham Forest. In 2006 alone, Brian and Gary planted 8,000 trees – mainly native oaks and other broadleaved hardwoods. This year they'll be adding another 2,000.

"There's no such thing as a typical day's work in this job," says Brian. "One day we could be planting trees, another maintaining fences or preparing the grounds for big outside events. We have 400 acres of forest to look after and the acreage is growing all the time as we plant trees in the corners of land that aren't very good for agriculture.

Brian lives with his wife, Diana, on the edge of the estate, in Cottingham. She also still works part-time, as a guide at Rockingham Castle.

The castle's owner, James Saunders Watson, says: "Brian contributes to the life of Rockingham in so many ways. He is our living encyclopaedia of knowledge of all aspects of the estate, with a remarkable memory for detail that we call on regularly. His understanding of trees is second to none and they are without doubt his great passion in life. He turns his hand to the many jobs that fall to him with enthusiasm and a smile. He epitomises the traditional countryman with interest in country life, the natural world, people and most of all his family."

Reviving an ancient craft

In Britain we're proud of our heritage and countless millions of pounds are spent every year preserving our great cathedrals and old buildings. Yet at the same time some of the most historic man-made structures in our area are crumbling before our eyes.

I'm talking about the dry stone walls that are such a feature of our area. Did you know that in our neck of the woods (Northamptonshire, Peterborough, North Cambridgeshire and South Lincolnshire) there are more stone walls than in Yorkshire? No, nor did I. Nor did I know that they are disappearing fast.

To make matters worse, there's only one man in this area qualified to build or repair them. Luckily that man is Richard Donoyou, who is on a one-man mission to ensure that there will soon be dozens of local people versed in the ancient craft of dry stone walling.

"We are losing the stone walls of the Nene valley at an alarming rate," says Richard. "Look at almost any village and you will find a wall in disrepair. The big estates , like Deene Park and Milton Park, for example, have a major challenge in keeping their miles and miles of historic walls in good repair.

"Look beneath many woodlands and hedgerows in this area and you'll find the remnants of stone walls that must have existed in good repair probably into the early 20th century. Until then, building and repairing dry stone walls was an important job in winter for farm and estate workers in the countryside, but after the first world war the labour force was massively reduced and the attitude of the large landowners changed. There just weren't the people available to manage and maintain them."

Richard, who lives in Elton, is a qualified building surveyor who admitted that he got bored sitting in front of a drawing board or computer screen and set about the task of learning traditional building techniques.

"I think it is important to get some practical understanding of these skills so one can appreciate the problems and benefits when asking others to employ them. So I have rebuilt timber frame houses, taught myself traditional slate roofing and thatching, and limestone dry stone walling, lime plastering and so on," he says.

His passion for the old building techniques is matched only by his determination to pass them on. He is currently teaching the art of dry stone walling to 17- and 18-year-old students at Peterborough Regional College and is about to start a series of courses aimed at adults who want to learn the craft.

"Some of our students haven't done well at school and left with no qualifications," he says. "This is a way of bringing them back into education, encouraging them to work as a team and improve their employment prospects. Many of them go on to learn other building techniques and will get jobs in the construction industry."

The courses take place both at the regional college and at John Clare's Cottage, Helpston, where the students are currently renovating a dry stone boundary wall that dates back to the early 18th century, when the famous poet lived there. In fact dry stone walls date back much further than that. The remains of Roman dry stone walls can be found at Church Hill, Castor, for example, while in Co Mayo in western Ireland, dry stone walls dating back 4,500 years have been uncovered by archaeologists.

The likelihood is that there is a dry stone wall very close to you. In fact you may have one on your property in need of repair – or you may even fancy building one. If so, Richard's courses for adults, which start in the spring, could be right up your street. "Following the success of the student courses, I am starting adult courses in March and April," says Richard. "We intend to offer week-long courses as well as weekend courses for those with full-time jobs.

"The courses would be suitable for builders and landscape contractors, estate workers, architects, building surveyors and conservation officers, as well as people who have stone walls in their gardens and around their houses which they wish to repair. A full week course should equip most people with sufficient skills to be able to progress by themselves. It is also intended that there will be further courses culminating in the Dry Stone Wall Association's First Level Certificate standard."

It is Richard's hope that one day there will be lots of qualified dry stone wallers in the area to ensure that these important features of our landscape are preserved for ever.

Dry stone walls are common in this area because of the ample supplies of limestone, literally under our feet. It is known as Oolitic limestone, laid down in the Jurassic period some 150 million years ago. The stone was formed as small invertebrate creatures died and fell to the bottom of the shallow tropical seas that existed at that time. Their calcareous shells then built up in layers, with each successive layer crushed to form the strata that is characteristic of limestone. As one works with the stone, the imprints of ancient plant fronds, large whelk like crustaceans and even trilobites can be found.

"Oolitic limestone is a wonderful building stone that has a consistency that allows it to be shaped and carved and a wonderful honey coloured hue," says Richard. "It was so highly valued by the Normans that its use was limited only to the church and the very wealthy.

"The quarries at Barnack produced particularly good stone and so became controlled by the church and the stone was used exclusively for great building projects including Peterborough and Ely cathedrals. Other dry stone boundary walls clearly have medieval origins. For example the wall that weaves and twists along the southern side of Sulehay Wood clearly marks a characteristic medieval boundary."

All the fun of the Feast

What have the patron saint of pilgrims and the village of Thurning got in common? The answer can be found every July 25th when the residents of the village, near Oundle, get together for the Feast of St James. It's something they've been doing in Thurning for hundreds of years – and the good news is that you can join the fun too, for free.

Unlike a lot of old country traditions that have been allowed to die out, Thurning Feast has been updated and improved over the years by generations of enthusiastic villagers to keep it relevant to contemporary tastes. Recent Thurning feasts have featured appearances by the Dead Rabbits – the UK's only Pogues tribute band – as well as the Nassington and Yarwell Brass Band, the Thurning Skiffle Band, an old-time Cajun and Blue Grass band... and a succession of talented local dancers and musicians.

Forget Britain's Got Talent. Thurning has got it in spades.

The event usually kicks off in the field opposite the village church with a typical village fete atmosphere, complete with rides for the kids, hog roast, beer tent, crafts and bric-a-brac stalls. But as the sun sets lower in the sky, the temperature rises as the live acts begin... and continue through to the small hours.

The organisers of this rural extravaganza are father and son team, Derek and Justin Capp. Justin, former landlord of the King's Arms pub at nearby Polebrook, says: "It's a modern twist on an old tradition and there's something for everyone. Our aim is for everyone to have fun. It's free parking and free entry. The only thing we ask is that people don't bring their own food and drink, but support the refreshment stalls and beer tent. The people of Thurning have been letting their hair down at St James Feast since Medieval times. Having fun is the most important part – and let's face it, it's not often you get to see six live bands performing and don't have to pay anything."

Thurning is believed to be on the route of pilgrims from northern England heading for the shrine of Saint James, in north-west Spain. James was one of the 12 Disciples and is the patron saint of pilgrims and labourers. After spreading the gospel in Spain after the death of Jesus, he returned to Judea, where he was arrested and executed by King Herod. His remains were taken to Spain and buried near Santiago, where his shrine is still visited every year by thousands of pilgrims. Thurning's parish church is dedicated to Saint James.

Thurning Feast dates back 800 years, although 'attractions' in past centuries would have been extremely gory to modern tastes, as they often involved cruel acts to animals. "There are still old people in the village who can remember when a live chicken would be suspended upside-down from a tree and to attempt to win it you would be blindfolded and try to cut its head off with shears," says Justin, with a shudder. "These days we just stick to good, clean fun..."

Where there's muck...

We all recycle these days. We fill our plastic bins of various colours and as if by magic those nice men from the council come along and take it away. It's our way of doing what's right for the planet, isn't it? But how many of us give a thought to what happens to our bottles, cartons, newspapers and cans after they disappear round the corner at the end of the street? As it happens, quite a lot happens to it when it turns up at Peterborough City Council's Material Recycling Facility at Fourth Drove, Fengate, A lot more than I ever imagined, anyway.

Inside a huge, hangar-like building on the very edge of the city, lorries arrive around the clock depositing huge loads of the items we put in our green bins. These are shovelled by machinery onto a bewildering tangle of conveyor belts, revolving drums, magnets and blasts of compressed air – in fact all manner of high-tech machinery – to sort the plastic from the glass, the paper from the cardboard and the steel from the aluminium.

Drinks cans, old newspapers, magazines, junk mail, plastic bottles, cardboard cartons and broken glass whizz past at lightning speed. Yet a team of eagle-eyed workers hover over it all, snatching out the rogue items that should never have been placed in the recycling bin the first place.

Nigel Wright, the facility manager, makes a lunge for a half-empty paint tin that's shooting by, almost concealed among a pile of yesterday's papers. "Stuff like this could contaminate a whole batch of material and make it useless for recycling," he explains. "If the can burst open, the paint would get everywhere and the whole lot would have to go to landfill. It really is important that householders put the right stuff goes in the recycling bin."

The worst contaminant is old engine oil. The commonest is supermarket plastic bags, which can clog up the machinery. The most dangerous to the 70 staff that work round the clock here are discarded needles. The workers wear thick leather gloves, but there's always the fear of a scratch from an HIV-infected syringe.

Even firearms and rounds of ammunition have been found. The most tragic find was the tiny body of a dead baby girl, two years ago, but dead household pets – particularly cats – are commonplace. It's astonishing to imagine somebody putting out their dead moggie for recycling... recycling into what exactly?

Yet Nigel doesn't berate the selfish or ignorant households that put the wrong stuff in their bins and make his work more difficult. He's genuinely enthusiastic about waste management in general and recycling in particular. And he wants others to share his ideals. It is, after all, in all our interests.

To encourage councils to recycle, the Government levies an ever-increasing tax on waste that goes to landfill. The more waste that is successfully recycled, the less the council has to pay in landfill tax and the less we have to pay in council tax. And that's quite apart from the good we're doing the planet.

Where there's muck there's brass, they say. And nowhere is that more true than in the recycling industry, which is truly a multi-million pound industry. Peterborough's recycling facility is run by Viridor, one of the big national players with recycling plants all over the country. It also has a central sales team that sells the recycled waste.

An average day at Fengate sees 250 to 300 tons arrive. Around 90 per cent of that is successfully recycled and packaged into bales, weighing three-quarters of a ton apiece. These are then sold on. Mixed paper, newspapers and pamphlets, cardboard and plastics go to re-processing sites at home and abroad, while aluminium and steel cans and glass go to UK re-processors.

In our consumer-driven throwaway society, we're running out of landfill sites to dump all the stuff we chuck out. We're also running out of the raw materials that are needed to create that stuff in the first place, so it makes sense to recycle what we can.

As befitting an environment city, Peterborough has a recycling record to be proud of, but it isn't resting on its laurels. The city council has already bought an empty factory next door to the recycling plant, which means it will roughly double in size in the next year or so. And, to encourage more people to recycle properly, it is embarking on an educational campaign.

A spokesman for the council explained that Peterborough is a diverse city with many ethnic groups and an estimated 73 languages spoken. Some have a poor command of English and it is difficult to get the recycling message across to people who don't understand what you're saying. The council is therefore appointing bilingual council officers to help drive the message home.

It is a message that Nigel Wright is happy to repeat to anyone he can. His enthusiasm is infectious and makes you want to rush home and recycle something. With an almost missionary zeal, he explains how we can all help make the world a better place for future generations. "In 30 years time I want to be able to look my children in the eye and say 'I've tried to do my bit'," he says. "That's how important recycling is."

You were only supposed to blow the doors off...

Research shows that moving house is one of the most stressful life events, right up at the top with divorce and bereavement. So how would you like to do it every day... and be responsible for moving priceless artefacts worth tens of thousands of pounds?

That's what Paul Monks has been doing for a living for the last 27 years, but you'd be hard pressed to find a less stressed bloke. He travels all over the world, moving valuable antiques and works of art – and you know what? He loves every minute of it.

"My job's 50 per cent common sense and 50 per cent experience," says Paul, from Barnwell. "It's different to ordinary removals in that you can't just grab an item and stick it in the back of a van. Every item is different and you have to work out the safest way of transporting it. For example, some antique furniture has delicate legs, so you place it upside-down. I use high-quality blankets to wrap every item, which is then strapped with soft webbing to the side of the van. Depending on what I'm carrying, a load could be worth millions of pounds."

It might also be a long journey. Paul regularly makes trips to the Middle East and Far East for rich clients. He has also worked for some very famous ones. Professional discretion means he can't reveal some of his assignments, but his anecdotes include delivering an antique sideboard to singer Rod Stewart, who answered the door wearing a Celtic tracksuit, and taking a full-size gypsy caravan to the house of one of the Bee Gees.

On another occasion he delivered a pair of eight-foot-long whale tusks and an ostrich egg to the United Arab Emirates ambassador's residence in London. "I was terrified of braking sharply in case the egg cracked," he recalls.

Paul's worst – and most bizarre – experience was on a trip to Paris with a vanload of valuable antiques for a world-famous antiques house. Arriving in French capital in the evening, he parked overnight in a side street near his hotel and awoke the next morning to find the van missing.

"It turned out that I had parked outside the Algerian embassy and the police, concerned that the van could be a terrorist threat, had carried out a controlled explosion then towed it away. The windows were blown out and the doors blown off the hinges but, incredibly, the antiques in the back were unscathed. I was so relieved," says Paul, who is married with a grown-up daughter.

Paul entered the world of fine arts removals at 16, when he left school in his native Leeds. "It was the first job I applied for and I got it," he recalls. "It's a fantastic job – I've travelled all over the world, including America and Australia." His reputation for the safe transit of valuable and delicate objects means that increasingly his services are called upon for moving high-tech office equipment like computers and electronics. Paul's awkward loads include a grand piano that had to be taken up an escalator at the Sheraton Hotel in Dubai. His least favourite consignments are garden statues and marble ornaments – very heavy and delicate – but if you ask him nicely he'll still move them for you.

Posh and Proud

It all began very humbly, on May 17th, 1934. At a meeting at the former Angel Hotel in Bridge Street, Peterborough United Football Club was formed by a group of local fans. They were determined to set up a professional club in the city following the collapse of the earlier Peterborough and Fletton FC, which had folded in 1932 with debts of £250.

Back then, the club's ambitions were modest. Chairman Jack Swain said at the time that the goal was to join the Football League. It's all a far cry from today, with Peterborough United owned by one of Ireland's richest businessmen and led by the son of Britain's most successful manager. Their stated ambition is to take the club to the heady heights of the Premiership.

If they succeed, it will be some accomplishment. At the start of the 2007-08 season, Peterborough – nicknamed the Posh – were where they have languished for most of the past 47 years, in the basement of the English Football League. To get to the Premiership and dine at the game's top table, they had to win promotion from League Two, then League One and, finally, the Championship.

At the time of writing, in 2012, they have already arrived in the Championship – and survived their first season there. So who knows?

Don't laugh. While the world of football is full of hopeful hype and dashed ambitions, Peterborough United is different. Owner MacAnthony is a 36-year-old property tycoon who has put his money where his mouth is to give manager Darren Ferguson the funds he needs to turn the dream into reality.

Ferguson, of course, is the son of Britain's most successful football manager, bar none. Sir Alec Ferguson has been at the helm of the world's biggest football club, Manchester United, for more than a quarter of a century, in which they have scaled unprecedented heights. And football fans of Peterborough United are praying that the Ferguson family magic has rubbed off on his son. If they succeed, it will be just reward for the long-suffering supporters of the club, who have experienced a roller-coaster ride over the years. And it will be good news for football-mad youngsters in the city, for MacAnthony is determined to portray supporting The Posh as a cool thing to do.

But to truly buy into the Peterborough United experience, you have to appreciate the history of a club that has seen triumph and despair in equal measure over the decades. Peterborough United kicked off in the old Midland League on September 1st, 1934. The London Road ground was owned by the city council, and basic to say the least, but fund-raising efforts by supporters over the years improved amenities.

Twenty years later, the club raised enough cash to buy the ground off the council and improve facilities, with new terracing and covered stands. At around the same time, the little non-league club gained a reputation for giant-killing, beating several much bigger and famous clubs in the annual FA Cup competition. But in those days the league was very much a closed shop and it wasn't until 1960 that Posh were finally elected to what was then Division Four. They didn't stay there long. In their very first season they won the championship and were promoted to Division Three. In 1965, Peterborough beat the mighty Arsenal in the FA Cup and the club was very much in the ascendancy. In the 1966-67 season The Posh looked likely for promotion to Division Two, but disaster struck when they were found guilty of financial irregularities – ie making illegal payments, known in the game these days as 'bungs' – and by way of punishment were relegated to Division Four instead.

Those were the dark years and there they languished until 1972 when the legendary Noel Cantwell was appointed manager. The following season he led them back to Division Three, where they stayed until 1979... when they were again relegated to the bottom division. Despite a few near-misses, they stayed rooted there until 1991 – an unproductive era brightened only by a few more giant-killing acts, including the scalp of West Bromwich Albion in the Littlewoods Cup in 1988.

That remarkable promotion season of 1990-91 had begun with former Liverpool star (and current BBC Match of the Day pundit) Mark Lawrenson as manager, who was replaced a few months later by former Posh player Chris Turner – a man who veteran Peterborough United fans still regard as the club's greatest-ever servant. The next season, Turner went one better and led Peterborough to the second flight of English football for the first time in the club's history, after winning the play-off final against Stockport at Wembley Stadium.

Had The Posh finally hit the big time? Well, nearly. In what was then League Division One they finished 10th in their first season (1992-93), beating local rivals Leicester City 3-0 in the process, but the following season they experienced that all-too-familiar sinking feeling as they were relegated back to Division Two.

Since then, the club has yo-yoed between the two bottom divisions. The most excitement in that time has been in the boardroom. Notable owners of the club have included local businessman and pizza baron, Peter Boizot, and the controversial Barry Fry, who first arrived as manager before eventually buying the club.

In truth, during this era the club became something of a soap opera. Fry was never shy of publicity and appeared twice on national TV in fly-on-the-wall documentaries that did nothing to enhance the reputation of Peterborough United. Glimpsing behind the scenes of the testosterone-fuelled world of professional football is never a pretty sight – and the foul language and temper tantrums of the dressing room were always likely to deter people from attending matches.

Peterborough United also hit the headlines in 2002 when the club's attempt to register the brand 'Posh' was disputed by none other than Victoria Beckham, former Posh Spice wife of England captain, David. It was a trivial diversion that put a much-needed smile on the faces of the long-suffering fans.

Stars who made their debut at Peterborough United included former England goalkeeper, David Seaman, who joined the club in 1982 after being rejected by Leeds United! He was sold to Birmingham City two years later for £100,000.

Another fans' favourite was former Wolves and Northern Ireland international, Derek Doogan, who played for the club from 1963-65. The most-loved player (and manager) in the club's history was Chris Turner, who played 357 games between 1969-78. Despite being a defender, he scored 40 goals in the process.

In September 1976, football legends George Best, Bobby Moore and Rodney Marsh appeared for Fulham in a League Cup tie against The Posh at London Road, which Peterborough lost 2-1.

The youngest player ever to play for the club was future Spurs star, Matthew Etherington, who was just 15 and a pupil at the city's Deacon's School when he made his debut against Brentford in 1997.

A fan's tale (and a legend's memories)

One day in 1958, a 13-year-old boy bought a ticket at Thrapston Station and boarded a steam train to Peterborough East Station. From there, it was a short walk to the turnstiles at London Road. And that day he became a lifelong Posh fan. More than half a century on, the stations are long demolished and steam trains but a distant memory. But Vic Morehen is still a dedicated follower of his favourite team.

"I can't remember why I became a Peterborough United fan," he says. "We lived in Islip, halfway between Peterborough and Northampton, and a lot of my mates became Cobblers (Northampton Town) fans. But I supported the Posh – and still do."

Vic can remember when Peterborough were elected to the Football League in 1960. He was there in the crowd when they demolished Arsenal in the FA Cup, in 1965. But he was also there when they were relegated in disgrace in 1968 for making illegal bonus payments... and he was still there throughout the lean 1980s when Posh languished in football's basement Division 4.

"When you support a club, you support them through thick and thin – good times and bad," says Vic, who is a season ticket holder. People talk about them making it to the Premier League, but the first priority to stay in the Championship. Whatever happens, I'll always support the Posh."

Vic says Peterborough United's finest hour came on January 30th, 1965. The occasion was the fourth round of the FA Cup. The opponents: Arsenal. Peterborough United have always boasted a giant-killing reputation, but this 2-1 win more than half a century ago was their finest hour.

Posh conceded an early goal to the visitors, but the legendary Northern Ireland striker Derek Doogan equalised before winger Peter McNamee scored the winner in front of an ecstatic crowd of 30,056 who had squeezed into the London Road ground.

It was the most important goal ever for Peterborough – and for Peter himself. "How can you ever forget a moment like that?" he recalls. "It has to be the most special goal I ever scored – although I did score another one very special one against Aston Villa in front of a capacity crowd at Villa Park."

Scottish-born Peter joined Posh in 1954, after he had finished his National Service in the Army, and stayed with the club until 1967. Aged 74, he still lives in Peterborough, and is a great fan of all sports - especially golf, which he plays on a regular basis.

"It was a great life as a footballer, but of course we didn't the money they get these days. I was paid £20 a week, with a £4 bonus if we won," he recalls.

For Arsenal, managed by former England captain Billy Wright, the match was one of the most embarrassing defeats in their history and Wright – who as a player had been the first to win 100 England caps – resigned at the end of the season.

The Ups and Downs of Peterborough United

1934-35: Peterborough United Football Club is formed and joins the Midland League. A crowd of 4033 turns out for Peterborough's first match – a 4-0 win over Gainsborough Trinity on September 1st, 1935.
1946-47: Posh suffer their worst-ever FA Cup defeat – 8-1 to local rivals Northampton Town in the second round.
1956-57: Peterborough's first FA Cup giant-killing act – a 5-4 victory over second division Lincoln City in a third round replay.
1957-58: Posh hit the FA Cup trail again, holding mighty Fulham to a draw in the third round before narrowly losing the replay.
1958-59: More FA Cup shocks as Posh defeat Shrewsbury, Walsall and Ipswich before falling to Sheffield Wednesday in the fourth round.
1960-61: Gain admission to the Football League. Score 134 goals in their first season – an all-time record by an English club. Striker Terry Bly grabs 52 of them (another record). Win Division 4.
1961-62: Beat Newcastle United before exiting the FA Cup in round four, to Sheffield United.

1964-65: Beat Arsenal in the FA Cup before falling to Chelsea in the quarter-finals.

1967-68: Finish ninth in Division 3, but demoted to Division 4 for making illegal bonus payments to players.

1973-74: Promoted from Division 4 as champions.

1975-76: Lose 3-1 in the fourth round of the FA Cup to Manchester United in front of a 56,352 crowd at Old Trafford.

1978-79: Relegated to Division 4 (where they are to remain for more than a decade).

1985-86: Suffer record league defeat – 7-0 to Tranmere Rovers.

1990-91: Promoted from Division 4 to Division 3.

1991-92: Promoted via play-offs to Division 1.

1993-94: Relegated to Division 2.

1996-97: Relegated to Division 3

1993-94: Peterborough hold Tottenham Hotspur to a 1-1 draw in the third round of the FA Cup, but lose 5-4 in the replay at White Hart Lane.

1999-2000: Promoted to Division 2, via play-offs.

2004-05: Relegated to League Two.

2007-08: Runners-up in League Two; promoted to League One

2008-09: Runners-up in League One; promoted to the Championship

Finally, why are they called 'The Posh'? Amazingly, the nickname has been around longer than the club, dating back to 1921 when Pat Tirrel, player-manager of Fletton United, announced that he was looking for "posh players for a posh team". The name stuck – even after Fletton United folded in 1932 – two years before Peterborough United was formed.

And finally...

I hope you've enjoyed the tales in this book. If it has helped you better appreciate our special corner of the kingdom, then all the better. It's just a short journey from the vibrant city that is modern Peterborough to the unspoilt countryside and lovely villages of the Nene valley and Rockingham Forest – much of which has remained largely unchanged for centuries. Long may it remain so.

David Phillips

Printed in Great Britain
by Amazon

72971474R00088